Robert A. S. Macalister

Ecclesiastical Vestments

their development and history

Robert A. S. Macalister

Ecclesiastical Vestments

their development and history

ISBN/EAN: 9783337332006

Printed in Europe, USA, Canada, Australia, Japan

Cover: Foto ©Lupo / pixelio.de

More available books at **www.hansebooks.com**

THE CAMDEN LIBRARY

ECCLESIASTICAL VESTMENTS:

Their Development and History

BY

R. A. S. MACALISTER, M.A.

Member of the Royal Society of Antiquaries of Ireland

LONDON :
ELLIOT STOCK, 62, PATERNOSTER ROW
1896

PREFACE

WITHIN comparatively recent years the discovery has been made that it is possible to treat the Bible, for critical purposes, as though it were an ordinary item of national literature, while maintaining a fitting reverence for it as the inspired Word; and that by so doing a flood of sidelight is cast upon it which illuminates the obscurity of some of its most difficult passages.

So, to compare lesser things with greater, it is possible and advisable to discard all feeling of ecclesiasticism (so to term it) when speaking of ecclesiastical antiquities. The science of ecclesiology is of comparatively recent growth, and it has hitherto suffered much at the hands of those who have approached it not so much to learn the plain lessons it teaches, as to force it to declare the existence or non-existence in early or mediaeval times of certain rites and observances. While we should treat ancient churches and their furniture with respect—a respect which should not be denied to the despised, though often quaint and interesting, high pews and west galleries— as being edifices or instruments formed for the use of the worshippers of God, yet for antiquarian purposes they should be examined and dissected in exactly the same spirit as that in which we investigate the temples of ancient Greece, or the stone weapons of prehistoric man. In this spirit the author of the present book has worked.

Ecclesiology, besides its sentimental connection with ecclesiasticism, possesses many features which render it the most popular branch of the great all-embracing science of archaeology. The objects with which it is concerned appeal strongly to the senses ; the finest works of the architect, the limner, the silversmith, the engraver, the embroiderer, the illuminator, and the musician, come within its scope ; they are accessible to all who live within reach of an ancient church or a moderately good museum, and the pleasant excursions and companionships with which its votaries are favoured invest its pursuit with the happiest associations. Above all, it lacks that terrible obstacle which lies at the threshold of almost every other subject of serious archaeological study — the necessity of attaining perfection in at least one foreign language. No one can form more than the merest *dilettante* acquaintance with the antiquities of India, Egypt, Greece, Ireland, or any other country, without mastering the language in which the records of the country are written ; but the merest smattering of mediaeval dog-Latin is quite sufficient to open the door to high (not, perhaps, *the highest*) attainments in ecclesiology.

These manifold attractions have resulted in hampering the study of ecclesiology with a serious drawback, which is wanting in nearly all the other branches of archaeology. The investigation of the marvellous antiquities of the four countries just mentioned—or, indeed, of almost any other country—can be undertaken by a student with the certainty that if he applies himself to it sufficiently to master the many difficulties which will, no doubt, present themselves, he will be in a position to break ground as yet untouched ; his knowledge will enable him to make original discoveries of his own. But it is far otherwise in ecclesiology. So easily understood are the facts of the subject (except in a few obscure points relating to the early Church) ; so definite are the statements of the numberless records, when the vagaries of symbolical theorizers are sifted away from them ; so countless has been, and is, the army of students, that the scope for research-work is reduced to a minimum ; hardly anything is left for the originally-minded worker but to discover the personal names of the different artists whose handiworks he sees before him, or else to propound some startling and revolutionary theory respecting the use of low-side windows or Easter sepulchres.

In the subdivision of ecclesiology with which this book is concerned, originality, whether of fact or treatment, is practically impossible. This work cannot claim to be more than a compilation, but it can claim to fill a space not exactly occupied by any other book, in that it gives in a brief and convenient form the principal facts connected with vestments and their use throughout the chief subdivisions of the Christian Church; it is not, as are almost all other works on the subject, confined to one branch only, or at most to the great Churches of the West and the East, but includes as well the smaller and more isolated communities, and those branches of the Universal Church which have undergone reformation.

Exception may possibly be taken to the manner in which the alleged symbolism of vestments has been treated. But it is impossible to overlook the facts. If, as is now the opinion of every leading ecclesiologist, the vestments are the natural result of evolution from civil Roman costume, it is clearly ludicrous to suppose that when they were first worn they possessed the symbolical meanings they are alleged to bear; the symbolism is as much an accretion as are the jewels and the embroidery of the middle ages. Moreover, the symbolical meanings attached to them are so obviously the 'private judgments' of the writers who describe them, and are so irreconcilable and so far-fetched, that to the unbiased mind they do not appear worthy of serious treatment.

In some recent books on ecclesiological and antiquarian matters Greek words are transliterated into English characters. This practice has not been followed in the present work because of the unsatisfactory appearance of Greek words in Roman dress, and because the Greek alphabet is familiar to all students. Words of other languages, such as Russian or Armenian, are, however, expressed in English letters, as their alphabets are not so well known, and they are not so easily set up in native type.

I must record my indebtedness to my lamented friend the late Prof. Middleton for useful hints and assistance; to Dr F. R. Fairbank, of St Leonard's-on-Sea, for many notes and references which have been of great value to me, and especially for the loan of several blocks; to Mr W. J. Kaye for the loan of a rubbing of the Sessay brass; to the Rev. S. Schechter for kind assistance in questions which arose in the first chapter; to the Rev. A. D. A. van Scheltema for information regarding the Church of Holland; and for many helps and suggestions to my father, to whom, in acknowledgment of the interest he has throughout shown in the preparation of the book, I wish to dedicate it. A list of the principal works laid under contribution is given in an Appendix.

R. A. S. M.

CONTENTS

CHAPTER I.

THE GENESIS OF ECCLESIASTICAL VESTMENTS - 1

PAGE

CHAPTER II.

THE EARLY DEVELOPMENT OF ECCLESIASTICAL VESTMENTS IN THE WESTERN CHURCH - - 24

CHAPTER III.

THE FINAL FORM OF VESTMENTS IN THE WESTERN CHURCH - - - - - 60

CHAPTER IV.

THE HISTORY AND CHARACTERISTICS OF THE PROCESSIONAL VESTMENTS; THE ORNAMENTATION OF VESTMENTS - - - - - 137

CHAPTER V.

THE VESTMENTS OF THE EASTERN CHURCHES - 175

CHAPTER VI.

THE VESTMENTS OF THE REFORMED CHURCHES - 192

CHAPTER VII.

THE RITUAL USES OF VESTMENTS - - - 211

APPENDIX I.

COSTUMES OF THE RELIGIOUS ORDERS - 235
MEDIAEVAL UNIVERSITY COSTUME - - - 253

APPENDIX II.

AN INDEX OF SYNONYMOUS TERMS - - - 257

APPENDIX III.

A LIST OF THE PRINCIPAL AUTHORITIES REFERRED
TO IN THE COMPILATION OF THIS WORK - 258

INDEX - - - - - - 262

LIST OF ILLUSTRATIONS

(*For full titles of sources followed see Appendix III*)

FIG.   PAGE

BRASS OF SIMON DE WENSLAGH, WENSLEY, YORKS *Frontispiece*

1. VESTMENTS OF THE JEWISH PRIESTHOOD. (*After Bock*) - - - - - - 5
2. BISHOP ADMINISTERING BAPTISM. (*Marriott*) - 37
3. ECCLESIASTICS FROM THE MOSAICS IN S VITALE, RAVENNA. (*Rock*) - - - - 46
4. EFFIGY OF A ROMAN CITIZEN IN CAERLEON MUSEUM. (*Bloxam*) - - - - 49
5. POPE GREGORY THE GREAT WITH PASTORAL STAFF. (*Smith and Cheetham*) - - 57
6. STOLE-ENDS, SHOWING VARIETIES IN FORM AND ORNAMENT. (*Archæological Association Journal*) - - - - - 73
7. ARCHBISHOP STIGAND, FROM THE BAYEUX TAPESTRY. (*Willemin*) - - - 76
8. DEACON IN EPISCOPAL DALMATIC. (*Building News*) - - - - - 78
9. DEACON IN DIACONAL DALMATIC. (*Rock*) - 78
10. SIR PETER LEGH, KNIGHT AND PRIEST. (*Haines*) 84

List of Illustrations.

FIG.		PAGE
11.	BISHOP WAYNFLETE'S EPISCOPAL SANDAL. (*Rock*)	92
12.	S DUNSTAN (FROM A MS. IN THE COTTONIAN LIBRARY). (*Marriott*)	97
13.	MONUMENT OF ALBRECHT VON BRANDENBURG, MAYENCE	101
14.	BISHOP WAYNFLETE'S EPISCOPAL STOCKING. (*Rock*)	105
15.	FIGURE OF A POPE (*temp.* INNOCENT III). (*Rock*)	108
16.	A BISHOP, SALISBURY CATHEDRAL. (*Bloxam*)	117
17.	MONUMENT OF DIETHER VON ISENBURG, MAYENCE	117
18.	PASTORAL STAFF AND MITRA PRETIOSA. (*Bloxam*)	120
19.	BRASS OF ARCHDEACON MAGNUS, SESSAY, YORKSHIRE	147
20.	BRASS OF ROBERT BRASSIE, KING'S COLLEGE, CAMBRIDGE	150
21.	CHRYSOME CHILD. (*Haines*)	172
22.	A COPE-CHEST, YORK MINSTER. (*Archæological Association Journal*)	173
23.	ARMENIAN PRIEST. (*Fortescue*)	177
24.	MALABAR PRIEST. (*Howard*)	178
25-28.	ILLUSTRATIONS OF ECCLESIASTICS OF THE EASTERN CHURCH. (*King*)	179-185
29.	A SYNOD MEETING OF THE REFORMED CHURCH OF FRANCE. (*Quick*)	205
30.	DEACON IN FOLDED CHASUBLE, WELLS CATHEDRAL. (*Archæologia*)	216

ERRATA.

Page 47, line 2, *for* maniple *read* mappula.
Page 63, line 2, *for* Walfrid *read* Walafrid.
Page 74, line 1 of footnote, *for* Goodrich *read* Goodrick.
Page 77, line 3 of footnote, *for* Whittlesford read Milton.
Page 106, last line, *for* succinctorium *read* subcingulum (also called 'succinctorium').
Page 110, line 13, *for* bishops *read* ecclesiastics.

ECCLESIASTICAL VESTMENTS.

CHAPTER I.

THE GENESIS OF ECCLESIASTICAL VESTMENTS.

THE study of ecclesiastical history or antiquities can be pursued from either of two standpoints. We may take into account those essentially religious or theological elements which distinguish this subject from all other branches of antiquarian science, and keep them prominently before us during our investigations; or else, disregarding those elements more or less completely, we may consider the subject wholly from the point of view of the antiquary.

As a general rule, those investigators who lay stress on the *ecclesiastical* rather than on the *antiquarian* side of ecclesiology and its various subdivisions have been attracted to the study not so much by the intrinsic interest which, in some degree, every branch of archæology possesses, as by the wish to settle controversial questions relating to Church doctrine, usage, or discipline. This is especially true of the important section of ecclesiology with which these pages are concerned. There are two schools into which the students of Church vestments may be divided—the ritualistic and the antiquarian. Each strives to attain full knowledge of the subject, and the means employed by both schools are the same—the evidence drawn from a patient comparison of the works of authors and artists of successive periods. But while those of the purely antiquarian school regard the knowledge thus gained as in itself the chief end of their researches, those of the other consider it rather as a stepping-stone, leading to proofs of the Divine appointment of the use of vestments, and indicating regulations to govern the usage of vestments in the modern Church.

It is not surprising that the results of the investigations of two schools, having aims so diverse in view, should be mutually incompatible. According to the views of some members of the ritualistic school, the vestments of the Christian Church were modelled directly upon the vestments of the Jewish priesthood; and as minute instructions for the shapes and usage of the latter were laid down in the divinely-revealed laws of Moses, they thus claim an at least indirect Divine appointment for

The Genesis of Ecclesiastical Vestments. 3

the Christian vestments. The antiquarian party, on the other hand, are unanimous in holding that the vestments of the Christian Church were evolved, by a natural process, from the ordinary costume of a Roman citizen of the first or second century of our era.

The consideration of these two theories must first occupy our attention. Neither is absolutely correct; for, although the balance of probability is enormously in favour of the second view, yet this theory, in the form in which it is often stated, does not cover certain changes which were made in the textures, outlines, and number of the vestments while the Church was yet comparatively young. These changes were all introduced to assimilate, as far as possible, the Jewish and Christian systems; and thus it may be said that both views contain an element of truth.

The theory of a Levitical origin is the older of the two; in fact, it was the first, and for many years the only, solution proposed. We shall therefore at the outset devote a page or two to considering its merits. Very few, even among the students of the ritualistic school, now hold it absolutely. The weight of argument which can be brought to bear against it is so great that it is almost universally abandoned as untenable.

For comparative purposes, it will be necessary at this stage to introduce a short descriptive catalogue of the vestments of the Levitical priesthood, as prescribed in the Book of Exodus (chap. xxviii). Josephus ('Antiquities,' iii 7) is also a *locus classicus* on the subject, and some additional particulars from that source are here incorporated :

I. *The Drawers or 'Breeches' of Linen.*

II. *The Tunic of Linen* ('coat of fine linen,' Exod. xxviii 39).—Josephus tells us that this tunic was of fine linen or flax doubled; that it reached to the feet, fitting close to the body, and was furnished with tight sleeves. It was girded to the breast, a little above the level of the elbows, by

III. *The Girdle.*—This was a strip of linen which, according to Josephus, was four fingers broad ; according to Maimonides,* three fingers broad and thirty-two cubits long. It was wound many times round the body ; the ends were then tied over the breast and hung down to the feet, except when the priest was engaged in sacrifice or other service, in which case he threw it over his left shoulder, so that it should not impede him in his duty. It was elaborately embroidered with flowers, worked in scarlet, purple, and blue threads.

* Mishneh Torah, VIII, section *de vasis sanctuar.*, viii 19, where some other particulars are to be found regarding the textures of which the Jewish vestments were made, etc.

IV. *The Priest's Cap* ('bonnet,' Exod. xxviii 40).—This was an ordinary turban, fastened round the head. The description given by Josephus is clear and detailed. He says: 'Upon his head he wears a cap, not brought to a conic form nor encircling the whole head, but still covering more than half of it, which is called *mesnaemphthes*; and its make is such that it seemeth to be a crown [garland], being made of thick swathes, but the contexture is of linen, and it is doubled round many times and sewed together; besides which, a piece of fine linen covers the cap from the whole upper part, and reaches down to the forehead and hides the seams of the swathes, which otherwise would appear improperly.'*

FIG. 1.—VESTMENTS OF THE JEWISH PRIESTHOOD.

* Ὑπὲρ δὲ τῆς κεφάλης φορεῖ πῖλον ἄκωνον, οὐ διϊκνούμενον εἰς πᾶσαν αὐτὴν, ἀλλ' ἐπ' ὀλίγον, ὑπερβεβηκότα μέσης· καλεῖται μὲν μεσναεμφθής. τῇ δὲ κατασκευῇ τοιοῦτός ἐστιν ὡς στεφάνη δοκεῖν, ἐξ ὑφάσματος, λινέου ταινία πεποιημένη παχεῖα, καὶ γὰρ ἐπιπτυσσόμενον ῥάπτεται πολλάκις. ἔπειτα

These four vestments constituted the complete equipment of the ordinary Jewish priest, as prescribed in the Mosaic law. The high-priest, however, added four more, which were as follows :

V. *The Tunic of Blue* ('robe of the ephod,' Exod. xxviii 31).—This was a long garment which, according to some authorities, reached to the feet, but according to others to the knees only. It was woven in one piece, with an aperture through which the head of the wearer was passed ; this aperture was guarded by a binding or braid to prevent it from tearing. Round the lower hem of this garment were hung golden bells and models of pomegranates, alternating one with another. The meaning of this remarkable ornament is not clear, and several explanations have been advanced to account for it ; all, however, fanciful, and not worth recording here.

VI. *The Ephod*, which was at once the most elaborate and the most important of the Jewish vestments, is more fully described than any of the rest. The superiority of this vestment over the others is due to the part which it, and the breastplate intimately connected with it, played in the mysterious revelations by which the children of Israel were guided during the period of the

σινδὼν ἄνωθεν αὐτὸν ἐκπεριέρχεται διήκουσα μέχρι μετώπου, τήν τε ῥαφὴν τῆς ταινίας καὶ τὸ ἀπ' αὐτῆς ἀπρεπὲς καλύπτουσα —Translation from Whiston.

Theocracy. For us, however, it would be as irrelevant as it would be futile to speculate on the nature of the revelation, or the instrumentality of the ephod in indicating the Divine will to the priest. We are here concerned only with the ephod as an element in the equipment of the high-priest, with its shape, and with such particulars of its ritual use as we can find directly stated in the different authorities.

'The ephod,' says Josephus, was 'woven to the depth of a cubit, of several colours [gold, blue, purple, and scarlet are enumerated in Exodus]; it was made with sleeves also; nor did it appear to be at all differently made from a short coat.'* The vestment seems to have consisted of two pieces, a front and a back, which were buttoned together by two onyx stones, one on each shoulder, set in bezils or 'ouches,' and engraved with the names of the twelve tribes, six on one, six on the other. Round the waist was passed a girdle, which was an essential part of the vestment—indeed, Josephus tells us that the girdle and the ephod were sewn together. This girdle, which was made of materials similar to those which constituted the ephod, seems to have been embroidered elaborately with coloured threads.

* Ὑφανθεὶς ἐπὶ βάθος πηχυαῖον ἔκ τε χρωμάτων παντοίων καὶ χρυσοῦ συμπεποικιλμένου, . . . χειρίσι τε ἠσκημένος, καὶ τῷ παντὶ σχήματι χιτὼν εἶναι πεποιημένος.

The ritual uses of the ephod, even apart from its supernatural associations, are obscure. It is distinctly implied both in Exodus and by Josephus that the vestment was intended for the use of the high-priest alone; yet we find allusions scattered through the early historical books of the Old Testament which clearly indicate that it was worn by others as well. Thus, we read in 1 Sam. xxii 18 that Doeg, commanded by Saul to fall on the priests who had assisted David, 'slew . . . fourscore and five persons that did wear a linen ephod.' Again, Samuel, when a child in the service of the priests, 'ministered before the Lord . . . girded with a linen ephod' (1 Sam. ii 18). Further, we read that King David himself, when he escorted the ark from the house of Obed-Edom to Jerusalem, was 'girded with a linen ephod.' In these three passages we read of an ephod being worn by the minor priest, the acolyte, and the layman, for none of whom it was originally intended. The most probable explanation seems to be that the ephod, originally intended as a vestment for the high-priest alone, was gradually assumed, probably in a less elaborate form, by the minor priests as well—when or how we cannot say. This explanation assumes that the regulation was originally laid down as it stands in Exodus; but it is possible that the more stringent restrictions may not be earlier than the recension of Ezra.

We learn from the incidents of Gideon (Judg. viii 27) and of Micah (Judg. xvii 5 ; xviii 14 *et seq.*) that the ephod, or, rather, copies of it, early became objects of superstitious veneration. In the two latter passages quoted, as well as in Hos. v 4, the vestment is coupled with the teraphim or *penates*, to the worship of which the Israelites showed marked inclination at different periods of their history. It may be noticed in passing that Ephod, which signifies 'giver of oracles,' is used as a personal name (Num. xxxiv 23).

VII. *The Breastplate of the Ephod.*—This was a rectangular piece of cloth of the same material as the ephod. That it might the better hold the precious stones with which it was set, it was doubled, its shape when so treated being that of a perfect square, with a side of about nine inches long. The stones were twelve in number, and fixed in settings of gold, being arranged in four rows of three each. On each stone was engraved the name of one of the twelve tribes.

This breastplate was secured by two plaited or twisted chains of gold, fastened at the one end to the bezils of the shoulder-pieces of the ephod, at the other to rings of gold in the upper corners of the breastplate, and by two blue cords secured to rings of gold in the lower corners of the breastplate and in the sides of the ephod above the embroidered girdle. Josephus asserts that there was an aperture in the ephod immediately under the breastplate. For this statement there is no Scriptural authority; but it is possible that it is the record of a modification in the details of the vestment naturally evolved and established at some time subsequent to the institution of the vestment itself.

VIII. *The Mitre.* — This did not differ in essence from the head-dress of the priests except in one important respect—the addition of a gold plate, set on a lace of blue, and bearing the inscription, 'Holy to Jehovah.' Josephus does not mention this plate, but describes the mitre as a kind of triple tiara, surmounted by a flower-shaped cup of gold, and covering the turban proper.* This, however, is quite at variance with the original laws on the subject.

In one respect these vestments are similar to those which it will be our duty to describe in the following pages. Although there is no injunction on the subject in the Law, the Talmud states clearly that 'he who wears the vestments of the priests outside the temple does a thing forbidden.'

* Ὑπὲρ αὐτὸν δὲ συνερραμμένος ἕτερος ἐξ ὑακίνθου πεποικιλμένος, περιέρχεται δὲ στέφανος χρύσεος ἐπὶ τριστοιχίαν κεχαλκευμένος. θάλλει δ' ἐπ' αὐτῷ κάλυξ, χρύσεος τῇ σακχάρῳ βοτάνῃ παρ' ἡμῖν λεγομένῃ ἀπομεμιμημένος, ὕος δε κύαμον Ἑλλήνων.

The Genesis of Ecclesiastical Vestments.

It is admitted by almost all students that the vestments during the first six or eight centuries of the Christian era were of much greater simplicity than those of later times. The evidence of contemporary art is overwhelmingly opposed to any other view. This fact being admitted, we need not be surprised by finding that until the eighth or ninth century no attempt was made to trace any connection between the elaborate vestments which we have just described, and the vestments worn by those who ministered in the offices of Christian worship.

It is true that until the time we have mentioned Churchmen did not greatly trouble themselves with investigations into the history of the religion they professed or the ritual they performed. But it is also true that several authors before this date enumerate the Jewish vestments, and enter at length into the figurative meanings which they were alleged to bear; but not one of these refers to any supposed genealogical connection—if the expression be permissible—between the two systems. This would be inexplicable if the Christian vestments were actually derived from the Jewish; for not only would the resemblance between the two be obvious, but the tradition of the assumption by Christian clerics of the vestments originally instituted for the Jewish priesthood would still be fresh in the minds of the authors. Yet not only do these writers not point out any resemblance between the two: they even make use of words and phrases which point to considerable differences between the outward appearance of Jewish and Christian vesture.

Apart from these considerations, may we not ask with reason how the early Christians, a poor and persecuted sect, could possibly assume and maintain an elaborate and expensive system of vestments such as the Jewish? And if the assumption had been made after the days of persecution were past, surely some record of the transaction would have been preserved till our own day? We possess a tolerably full series of the acts and transactions of ecclesiastical courts in all parts of the known world from the earliest times—how is it that all record of such an important proceeding has perished?

The first hint of the idea of the Mosaic origin of the Christian vestments is given by Rabanus Maurus, Archbishop of Mainz, in his treatise 'De Institutione Clericorum,'* written about the year 850. In the first book of this tract he discusses each Christian vestment in turn, endeavouring to find parallels to some of them among the vestments of the Jewish priesthood, but without much success. The seed thus sown, however, rapidly bore fruit among subsequent writers, who expanded the theory with great elaboration.

* I, cap. xiv *et seq.* (Migne, 'Patrologia,' vol. cvii, col. 306).

The Genesis of Ecclesiastical Vestments. 13

Many of the identifications brought forward by some of the late writers are very far-fetched, and mutually contradictory. To these but little weight can be attributed. It is a significant fact that none of the writers who endeavour to find parallels between the two systems can discover an equivalent among the Jewish vestments for the chasuble. Now, if for each of the Christian vestments there existed a corresponding vestment among those of the Jews, it would be singular that the most important of the former should be unrepresented among the latter. The maniple, too, has no equivalent (this, however, is more intelligible, since that ornament was certainly a later introduction); while the amice is the only vestment that even the most ingenious can produce to represent the ephod, though the similarity between the two is of the slightest.

There is another important point which the advocates of a Mosaic origin for Christian vestments overlook. The early Christians certainly did borrow many details of their worship from the Jews who lived around them, and from whose religion many of them had been converted; but these details were taken not from the antiquated ritual of the temple worship, but from the synagogue worship, to which they had been accustomed. Now, the vestments which we have described above were appointed for the tabernacle worship and the temple worship, its direct successor, whereas no vestments were at any time or by any authority appointed for use in the synagogue worship ;* and hence the Christian vesture cannot be said to 'come directly' from the Jewish.

We have discussed the theory of a Levitical origin on purely *a priori* grounds, making only the slightest allusion to the vestments themselves as we find them in primitive times. In considering the second view, to which it is now time to turn, we shall adopt a different course. We shall first collect the main facts which can be discovered or deduced respecting vestments in the earliest centuries of Christianity, from the beginning till the rupture of the East and the West, and then discuss in detail the vestments as we find them in the succeeding period, which in all ecclesiastical matters was a period of transition, comparing each in turn with its hypothetical prototype among the civil costume of the Romans. The remainder of the present and the whole of the succeeding chapter will be devoted to this investigation.

The materials available for an inquiry into the vestment usage of the early Church are twofold : the incidental statements of contemporary authors, and the more direct information obtained from a

* Such a vestment as the *talith* is not here considered, for this is worn by all the worshippers alike, as well as by the officiating minister.

study of contemporary paintings and sculpture. We shall now discuss the results which follow from an examination of these sources.

The references in the earliest writers—even including those which have a very indirect bearing on the subject—are extremely few in number; and all passages which can possibly throw any light on the question have been eagerly sought out and called into evidence to support one theory or another. The two best-known passages are the statement of St Jerome: 'Holy worship hath one habit in the ministry, another in general use and common life';* and the yet more famous passage in the liturgy of St Clement, in which a rubric directs the priest to begin the service 'girded with a shining vesture.'† The phrase λαμπρὰν ἐσθῆτα μετενδὺς has been translated 'being girded with *his* " splendid " vestment,' a translation which the Greek cannot possibly bear; and this passage, coupled with the excerpt from Jerome just quoted, have been brought forward to testify that gorgeous vestments were in use even at the early times when those documents from which they have been extracted were written.

* Hieron. in Ezek., cap. xliv. 'Religio divina alterum habitum habet in ministerio alterum in usu vitaque communi.'

† Εὐξάμενος οὖν καθ' ἑαυτὸν ὁ ἀρχιερεὺς ἅμα τοῖς ἱερεῦσιν καὶ λαμπρὰν ἐσθῆτα μετενδὺς καὶ στὰς πρὸς τῷ θυσιαστηρίῳ τὸ τρόπαιον τοῦ σταυροῦ κατὰ τοῦ μετώπου τὸν χειρὶ ποιησάμενος εἰπάτω κ.τ.λ.

Mr. Marriott has carefully examined and commented on these and the other passages cited as authorities. He proves that the first passage given above is used in a context which shows that Jerome, though possibly he may have had Christian usage in his mind, was thinking primarily of Jewish usage; the second (which not improbably is an interpolation) does not specify a 'splendid' vesture, but a 'white' or 'shining' garment.

Mr. Marriott's inference from these and similar passages is 'that white was the colour appropriated in primitive times [*i.e.*, in the first four centuries] to the dress of the Christian ministry.' Though this view is preferable to the theory that the primitive vestments were of the same elaborate description as their mediæval successors, yet it does not altogether commend itself as following naturally from the authorities cited. It will be necessary to review these passages, for, as we shall endeavour to show, they are quite consistent with the third alternative : that *no* distinctive vestments were set apart for the exclusive use of the Christian minister during the first four centuries of the Christian era.

The third passage is also from Jerome. In another part of the same commentary as the last he writes : 'From all these things we learn that we ought not enter the Holy of Holies clad in our everyday garments and in whatever clothes we will, defiled as they are by the usage of common life; but with pure conscience and in pure garments we ought to hold the sacraments of the Lord.'*

The fourth passage is from Jerome's letter against the Pelagians, in which occur these remarkable words: 'You say, further, that gorgeousness of apparel or ornament is offensive to God. But, I ask, suppose I should wear a comelier tunic, wherein would it offend God? or if bishop, priest, deacon, and the rest of the church officers were to come forward dressed in white?'†

Only one other passage remains. This is the account of the charge preferred against Cyril, Bishop of Jerusalem, before the Emperor Constantius. It is narrated in Theodoret (Eccl. Hist., ii 27), and, not being worth quoting at length, may be briefly stated thus: Constantine had sent to Macarius, the then bishop, a sacred robe—ἱεράν στολήν—made of threads of gold, to be worn when administering baptism; Cyril had sold this robe to a stage-dancer, who wore it during a

* 'Per quae discimus non quotidianis et quibuslibet pro usu vitae communis pollutis vestibus nos ingredi debere in sancta sanctorum sed munda conscientia et mundis vestibus tenere Domini sacramenta.'—Hieron. in Ezek., cap. xliv.

† 'Adjungis gloriam vestium et ornamentorum Deo esse contrariam. Quae sunt rogo inimicitiae contra Deum si tunicam habuero mundiorem? si episcopus presbyter et diaconus et reliquus ordo ecclesiasticus in administratione sacrificiorum candida veste processerint?'—Hieron., Adv. Pelagianos, lib. i, cap. 9.

public exhibition. It was further stated that the stage-dancer had fallen while dancing and been fatally injured.

As the reader will see, these passages give but few data for deductions as to the vestment-usage in the early Church. There is no indication, for instance, in the passage from Theodoret of what sort the sacred robe in question was : it may just as well have been a splendid garment originally from some temple or other. The fact that the early Greek ecclesiastical writers do not use the word στολή to denote a sacred vestment further weakens the force of this anecdote as an argument. Only Germanus, Patriarch of Constantinople (early seventh century), supplies another instance, where he says: ἡ στολὴ τοῦ ἱερέως . . . κατὰ τὸν ποδήρη Ἀαρών ; and this latter passage can be explained away, as στολή refers here to Jewish vesture, in which connection it is also employed by the Septuagint.

On a careful and unbiased reading of these passages, it will be noticed that nothing is said which can be construed into denoting garments of a special prescribed shape, and that their colour is only specified by such indefinite words as λαμπρός and *candidus*.

It is also important to notice that although in the first and third of the passages cited from Jerome a more special mention is made of the

The Genesis of Ecclesiastical Vestments. 19

dress of the clergy, yet it is not straining the meaning of either of them to regard them as applying equally well to the dress of the lay worshippers. This, of course, would preclude the supposition that they deal with any special ritual observance. The second of these quotations, if translated into homely nineteenth-century language, resolves itself into a simple but strong injunction to all worshippers (not the minister only) to wear their Sunday clothes. Mr Marriott lays great stress on the passage in the letter against Pelagius; its testimony is one of the strongest arguments which he can bring forward to support his thesis, that it was specially appointed, in the primitive church, that white vestments (something like the modern surplice) should be worn by the minister. But Jerome does not say, 'Is God displeased *because* the officers of the church dressed *candida veste?*' but '*would* God be displeased *if* they were so vested?' The entire passage is hypothetical; and nothing is more clear than that Jerome was not contemplating any hard and fast rules.

We may dismiss the passage from the Clementine Liturgy with very few words. Λαμπρός, which the ritualists translate 'splendid,' in classical Greek always means 'bright, brilliant, radiant,'* and

* See Liddell and Scott, Greek Lexicon, edit. maj., *sub voce.*

is applied in Homer to the sun and stars. It is also applied, in the sense of 'bright,' to white clothes; indeed, we find in Polybius* (*flor. circa* 150 B.C.) this very phrase, λαμπρὰ ἐσθής, equivalent to the Roman *toga candida*. Other meanings are 'limpid' (of water), 'sonorous' (of the voice), 'fresh, vigorous' (of action), 'manifest,' 'illustrious,' 'munificent,' 'joyous,' 'splendid' (generally, in outward appearance, health, dress, language, etc.); but it never wears the definite meaning which we should expect were the word intended to be applied to a definite vesture. The λαμπρὰ ἐσθής of the Clementine Liturgy is, in short, a bright, clean robe, but no more an article of an exclusively ecclesiastical nature than is the 'fair white linen cloth' with which the rubric of the Anglican Communion Service directs the altar to be covered.

Another passage, somewhat later in date, may be cited as a type of a large class of passages very apt to mislead too credulous students. It is the Gaulish description of St Berignus cited by Lipomanus (de Vitis Sanctor., Ed. Surius, Venice, 1581, vol. vi, p. 4), 'Vidi quendam hominem peregrinum, capite tonso, cujus habitus differt ab habitu nostro, vitaque eius nostrae dissimilis est.' The context, however, makes it plain that secular, not religious, dress is intended.

* Polyb., 10, 5, 1.

The Genesis of Ecclesiastical Vestments. 21

And when we refer to the few early frescoes and mosaics which have come down to us from the primitive epoch, we find ecclesiastics, apostles, and Our Lord Himself, represented as habited in the tunic and toga or pallium of Roman everyday life.

We gather, therefore, from these scattered shreds of evidence that, during the first centuries of the Christian church, no vestments were definitely set apart for the exclusive use of the clergy who officiated at Divine service : that clergy and people wore the same style of vesture both in church and out, subject only to the accidental distinctions of quality and cleanliness.

Fashion in dress or ornament is subject to constant changes which, though perhaps individually trifling, in time amount to complete revolutions ; but the devotees of any religion, true or false, are by nature conservative of its doctrines or observances. Combined with the conclusions at which we have just arrived, these two universally recognised statements yield us presumptive evidence of the truth of the theory which views the Roman civil dress as the true progenitor of mediæval ecclesiastical costume. We have seen that at first the worshippers wore the same costume both at worship and at home. Fashion would slowly change unchecked from year to year, while ecclesiastical conservatism would retard such changes so far as they concerned the dress worn at Divine service : small differences would spring into existence between everyday dress and the dress of the worshipper, and these differences, at first hardly perceptible, would increase as the process went on, till the two styles of costume became sharply distinguished from one another.

Parallel cases are not wanting to show that this is not altogether mere random theorizing. For example, the ministers of the Reformed Church of Holland maintained, till comparatively recently, a picturesque fashion of dress over a century old, which they wore only when conducting Divine service.* Perhaps, however, the objection may be urged against this view of the case, that if the process were such as we have described, it should apply as well to the worshippers as to the minister : that they, as well as he, should wear service-robes. It is possible that this would actually have been the case had the church services maintained their most primitive form, as St Paul describes it in the First Epistle to the Corinthians : ' When ye come together, every one of you hath a psalm, hath a doctrine, hath a tongue, hath a revelation, hath an interpretation ';† that is, had all the worshippers maintained an equally prominent position

* See Chapter VI.
† 1 Cor. xiv 26.

instead of selecting one of their number to conduct their services. At it was, the outstanding position of the minister rendered his equipment especially liable to such stereotyping as we have imagined.

In the following chapter we shall submit the truth of this theory to a test. If the genesis of ecclesiastical vestments actually took place in some such manner as this, then the vestments as we find them described in the earliest writers ought to bear conspicuous points of resemblance to the civil costume of the Roman people during the first three Christian centuries. We shall now inquire whether this be so.

CHAPTER II.

THE EARLY DEVELOPMENT OF ECCLESIASTICAL VESTMENTS IN THE WESTERN CHURCH.

THE last chapter has carried us down to the end of the fourth century A.D. For some time back the Roman Empire had been showing signs of disintegration. Already the three sons of Constantine had divided the imperial power among themselves; but the rule thus severed had again been united in the person of Constantius. In 395, however, the emperor Theodosius died, and left the empire of the world to be parted between his two sons, Arcadius and Honorius.

It would be outside our scope to enter into the details of the far-reaching consequences of this great event. For our present purpose it is sufficient to state that, with the empire in which it had been born and nurtured, the church was divided into two parts, which were thenceforth to

Early Development of Vestments. 25

develop independently, now in parallel, now in widely divergent lines.

It will be convenient to regard the first chapter as dealing with the period between the institution of Christianity and the partition of the Roman Empire; and in the present chapter to discuss the interval between the latter event and the accession of Charles the Great. We thereby divide the history into two epochs of approximately four centuries each, with characteristics sufficiently well marked to distinguish one from the other. Following Marriott, we shall name the first the *primitive*, the second the *transitional* period. We have seen that there is no evidence that vestments of any definite form were prescribed for use during the former epoch; we shall see in the present chapter how vestment-usage rapidly developed in the churches of the West till it culminated in the gorgeous enrichment of mediæval times.

Although the differences between the vestments of the Western and the Eastern churches consist largely in matters of detail, they are sufficiently conspicuous, and their histories are sufficiently divergent, to render their independent treatment advisable. We shall therefore postpone the discussion of the latter till we have investigated the evolution and subsequent elaboration of the former.

The empire to which Honorius succeeded consisted of Italy, Spain, Gaul, and Britain. Although the evidence which is extant does not permit us to trace completely the history of vestments throughout this period, yet from scattered documents we are able to see that for the most part the development of ecclesiastical costume proceeded on the same lines throughout this vast area.

Ritual in matters of dress had rapidly been growing. Pope Celestine, who occupied the Roman See from 423 till 432, found it necessary to write a sharp letter to the Bishops of Vienne and Narbonne for 'devoting themselves rather to superstitious observances in dress than to purity of heart and faith.' Certain monks, it appears, had attained to episcopal rank, but had retained their ascetic costume. Some of Celestine's sentences are very striking in this connection; and although they refer primarily to out-door costume, we cannot but think that, in a later age, when the regulations governing the ritual uses of vestments had been formulated, and the vestments themselves had been elaborated to their ultimate form, the force of his words would have been somewhat modified. 'By dressing in a cloak [*pallium*],' he says, 'and by girding themselves with a girdle, they think to fulfil the truth of Scripture, not in the spirit, but in the letter. For if these precepts were given to the end that they should be obeyed in this wise, why do they not likewise that which follows, and carry burning lights in their hands as well as their pastoral staves? We should be distinguished from the common people, or from all others, by our learning, not by our dress; by our habit of life, not by our clothing; by the purity of our minds, not by the cut of our garments. For if we begin to introduce novelties, we shall trample under foot the usage which our fathers have handed down to us, and give place to vain superstitions.'

The fullest information on the subject of vestments during this period comes from Spain, in the oft-quoted acts of the fourth council of Toledo, which sat under the presidency of St Isidore of Seville in the year 633. Of the canons which were drawn up at this council that which is of the highest importance in this inquiry is the twenty-eighth, although it is not directly connected with vestment-usage. It provides for the case of a cleric who had been unjustly degraded from his order, and ordains that such a one, if he be found innocent in a subsequent synod, 'cannot be reinstated in his former position unless he regain his lost dignities before the altar, at the hands of a bishop. If he be a bishop, he must receive the *orarium*,* ring, and staff; if a priest, the *orarium*

* Throughout this chapter I have retained the Latin words *orarium*, *planeta* and *alba* in preference to the English translations 'stole,' 'chasuble,' and 'alb,' when treating of

and *planeta*; if a deacon, the *orarium* and *alba*; if a subdeacon, the paten and chalice, and similarly for the other orders—they must receive, on their restoration, whatever they received on their ordination.'*

On the principle which is all but universal, that the clergy of the higher orders added the insignia of the lower orders to those of their own, we are enabled by the help of this act to draw up a table of the vestments recognised in Spain, which shows at a glance the manner in which they were distributed among the different orders of clergy:

> *Alba*: worn by all alike.
> *Orarium*: worn by deacons, priests, and bishops.
> *Planeta*: worn by priests and bishops.
> *Ring and staff*: exclusively for bishops.

Some letters of Gregory the Great (Bishop of Rome 590-604) give us particulars relating to

---

the vestments of the early church. The two are not identical, and it is convenient to have a short method of distinguishing one from the other.

* 'Episcopus presbyter aut diaconus si a gradu suo iniuste deiectus in secunda synodo innocens reperiatur non potest esse quod fuerat nisi gradus amissos recipiat coram altario de manu episcopi; (si episcopus) orarium annulum et baculum; si presbyter orarium et planetam; si diaconus orarium et albam; si subdiaconus patenam et calicem; sic et reliqui gradus ea in reparationem sui recipiant quae cum ordinarentur perceperunt.' [The bracketed words have dropped out from the MS., but their restoration is certain and necessary.]

three other vestments not in general use throughout the church. These are the *dalmatica*, the *mappula*, and the *pallium*. Lastly, an anonymous MS. of uncertain date* enumerates the *pallium, casula, manualia, vestimentum, alba,* and *stola* as the vestments worn in the Gallican Church. It is to be regretted that none of the British authors of the period have preserved any record of contemporary vestment-usage in this country; we have, however, no reason to suppose that it differed from that of the Continent.

Let us now take each of the above vestments in order, and collect whatever information is obtainable upon their appearance and history, comparing each in turn with its supposed Roman prototype.

I. *The Alba.*—This word is the abbreviated form of the full name, *tunica alba*, by which a flowing tunic of white linen was denoted. It appears that the first use of this word as a technical term for a special robe is in a passage of Trebellius Pollio (in Claud., xiv, xvii), who

* This MS. is edited in Martene's Thesaurus Anecdotorum, vol. v, p. 86 *et seq.*, and extracts are made from it in Marriott's work, p. 204. The MS. was found in the monastery of St Martin at Autun, and is assigned by Martene to the sixth century, though on doubtful grounds. Marriott is probably correct in referring it to the tenth. As the vestments which it describes rather resemble those of the final period than of the transitional, we reserve its discussion till the following chapter.

speaks of an *alba subserica*, mentioned in a letter sent from Valerian to Zosimio, Procurator of Syria, about 260-270 A.D. In the 41st canon of the fourth council of Carthage (*circa* 400 A.D.)* we meet with the first use of this word in an ecclesiastical connection, in one of the earliest (if not *the* earliest) regulations ever passed to govern the ritual usage of vestments. This ordains that the deacon shall wear an *alba* only '*tempore oblationis tantum vel lectionis.*'

The constant evidence of contemporary pictures indicates that the *alba* was a long, full, and flowing vesture. In this respect it differed from the Mosaic tunic, on the one hand, and the mediæval alb on the other. Both these vestments fitted closely to the body for reasons of convenience, for a flowing tunic would obviously hamper the Levitical priest in the discharge of his sacrificial duties, and would not sit comfortably under the vestments with which it was overlaid in mediæval times.

Nearly two centuries after the fourth council of Carthage we find the first council of Narbonne (A.D. 589) enacting that 'neither deacon nor subdeacon, nor yet the lector, shall presume to put off his *alba* till after mass is over.'† To this

* Labbe, Sacrosancta Concilia (1671), vol. ii, col. 1203.

† 'Nec diaconus aut subdiaconus certe vel lector antequam missa consummetur alba se præsumat exuere.'—Concil. Narb., i, Labbe, vol. v, col. 1030 (misprinted 1020).

The Early Development of Vestments. 31

canon, which was clearly framed to check some tendency to irregularity that had become noticeable in the celebration of mass, we are indebted for two facts : first, that ritual usage in vestments was now firmly established ; and second, that the *alba* was the dress of the minor orders of clergy. This latter point is not clearly brought out in the Toletan canon already quoted.

Of the garments worn in everyday life by the Roman citizen, the innermost was the *tunica talaris*, or long tunic. This article of dress was white, usually of wool ; it was passed over the head and reached to the feet, the epithet *talaris* ('reaching to the ankles') being employed to distinguish it, as the tunic of ceremony, from the short tunics worn when freedom was required for active exertion.* It fitted tolerably closely to the body, though it was sufficiently loose to require a girdle to confine it. The tunics of senators and *equites* were distinguished by two bands of purple, in the former case broad (*lati clavi*), in the latter narrow (*angusti clavi*), which passed from the sides of the aperture for the head down to the lower hem of the garment.

A comparison of the ecclesiastical *tunica alba* with the civil *tunica talaris* will bring out some remarkable points of resemblance. Both were

* It was also possible and usual to gird up the *tunica talaris* for this purpose.

worn in the same manner, and both reached to the feet; it is true that the ecclesiastical dress was slightly fuller than the civil, but this was necessary, as room was required underneath the *alba* for the wearer's everyday dress. Further, we find ecclesiastics represented in ancient frescoes wearing *albae* which actually show ornaments disposed like the *clavi* of the *tunica talaris*. These *clavi* were early employed by the Christians to distinguish, by their relative width, the representations of Our Lord from those of the Apostles, or to discriminate between the figures of ecclesiastics of different orders.

It is also important to notice that the *alba* is invariably furnished with tight sleeves reaching to the wrist. The tunic was originally a sleeveless garment; but with the growth of luxury, a new kind provided with sleeves gradually came into favour. These two forms of tunic were distinguished by different names: the older or sleeveless tunic was called *colobium*, a Latinization of the Greek name κολόβιον;* and the latter or sleeved tunic was named *tunica manicata* or *tunica dalmatica*, from the name of the province to which its invention was ascribed.

In the early days of Rome the use of a *tunica dalmatica* stamped the wearer with the stigma of effeminacy and utter want of self-respect. The

* Derived from the adjective κολοβός, *docked, curtailed*, in reference to the shortened sleeves of the garment.

parents of Cornelius Scipio and of Fabius are said to have openly disgraced them in their boyhood, as a punishment *ad corrigendos mores*, by compelling them to appear in public in this attire. The despicable emperors Commodus and Elagabalus offended all persons of good taste by coming out before all the people in the same costume: the latter impudently calling himself another Scipio or Fabius, in reference to the incident just related.* This, however, cannot mean that the scandal lay in the adoption of the luxurious *tunica dalmatica* in preference to the *colobium* (for Rome in the time of Elagabalus was too deeply steeped in luxury and vice to feel shocked at an Emperor merely preferring an under-garment with sleeves to one without those appendages); it rather consisted in his neglecting to put on his *pallium*, or outer dress, over it. In fact, the *tunica dalmatica* must have quite ousted its severer rival in popular favour by the time of Elagabalus: for we find that in 258, only thirty-six years after the death of that emperor, St Cyprian of Carthage wore a *tunica dalmatica*, over which was a *byrrhus*, or cloak, when led out to martyrdom.† It is absurd to suppose that Cyprian, on such a solemn occasion,

* Lampridius in Commodo, cap. viii; in Elagab., cap. xxvi.
† Acta S Cyp., *prop. fin.* (Migne, Patrologia, vol. iii, col. 1504).

would have assumed a merely luxurious garment, and equally absurd to imagine that he would have worn ecclesiastical vestments at the time, as some commentators on the passage have held. There remains only one other alternative—that the *tunica dalmatica* was the form of tunic which was in regular use at the time, and this seems quite the most satisfactory hypothesis.

The most important mention of the *tunica dalmatica* in connection with ecclesiastical matters is in the decree of Sylvester, Bishop of Rome, 253-257. That prelate ordained 'that deacons should use the *dalmatica* in the church, and that their left hands should be covered with a cloth of mingled wool and linen.'* Various authors supplement this passage; thus, the anonymous author of the tract 'De Divinis Officiis,' formerly attributed to Alcuin, tells us that 'the use of *dalmaticae* was instituted by Pope Sylvester, for previously *colobia* had been worn.'†

Much importance has been attached to this decree. It is regarded as an additional and incontrovertible proof that ecclesiastical vestments

* 'Ut diaconi Dalmatica uterentur in ecclesia et pallio linostimo laeva eorum tegeretur.'—Anastasius Bibliothecarius de Vit. Pontif., § 35 (S Sylv.); Migne, Patrol., vol. cxxvii, 1514.

† 'Usus autem Dalmaticarum a B. Sylvestro Papa institutus est: nam antea colobiis utebantur.'— Pseudo-Alcuin de Div. Off., cap. xxxix; Migne, vol. ci, 1243.

were in use in the primitive church. But on examination, however, it will be found no more to bear such a construction than St Paul's request for his φαιλόνη. The ordinance merely shows that Sylvester had a laudable desire to improve the aesthetics of public worship, and, with this end in view, decreed that thenceforward ecclesiastics should all wear the *tunica dalmatica*—which had quite outgrown its early evil reputation, and must be admitted to have been a better-looking garment than the scanty and somewhat undignified *colobium*. It is not at all improbable that many of the clergy wore *dalmaticae* even before Sylvester's edict : in this case the edict would have the additional advantage of securing uniformity.

All attempts to set up the *dalmatica* as a separate vestment in early times fail hopelessly. It is unknown to the drafters of the Toletan canons, and no *early* representation of an ecclesiastic is extant having two vestments visible under the *planeta*.* This would certainly be the case if the two were independent vestments. It is true that St Isidore of Seville wrote, ' Dalmatica vestis primum in Dalmatia provincia Graecia texta est sacerdotalis, candida cum clavis ex purpura ;'† (the *dalmatica* is a priestly vestment first made in

* This does not apply to the city of Rome. See p. 54.
† Etymologiae, lib. xix, cap. xxii (Migne, lxxxii 635).

Dalmatia, a province of Greece, white with purple *clavi*); but the concluding words show that he was merely thinking of the *alba* under its more specific name, *dalmatica*.

A brief recapitulation of this somewhat lengthy argument may not be out of place. Two forms of tunic may be said to have contended one with another for the favour of the Roman people—the sleeveless *colobium* and the sleeved *dalmatica*. The latter ultimately gained the victory; and the decree of Pope Sylvester, commanding all ecclesiastics under his authority to assume it in place of the former, finally established its use in the church. Now, when we find that, two or three centuries after Sylvester's time, a vestment was worn by ecclesiastics in Divine service identical with the *tunica dalmatica* in almost every respect, even to the presence of the *clavi*, which (in the secular dress) indicated the rank of the wearer, it is only natural to regard the one as directly derived from the other.

There is one other point of importance in the history of this vestment in the transitional period. It was found that such a flowing garment as the *alba* seriously incommoded the priest on some occasions, particularly in administering baptism by immersion. Accordingly, an *alba* fitting closely to the body was invented for use on such occasions, and is represented in certain MS. illuminations,

The Early Development of Vestments. 37

particularly a ninth-century pontifical now in the St Minerva Library at Rome. The special importance of this point is due to the fact that this baptismal *alba* was probably the immediate parent of the mediaeval alb; the closer vestment being found more convenient on other occasions as well as that of baptism, and having gradually become

FIG. 2.—A BISHOP ADMINISTERING BAPTISM.

adopted in all the other offices of the Church as well.

II. *The Orarium.*—Both this vestment and the name by which it was known have given much trouble to scholars. The following list of the various derivations which have been suggested for the word *orarium* (arranged in order of probability) is not uninteresting:

1. *Ora*, because used to wipe the face.
2. *Orare*, because used in prayer.
3. ὥρα, because it indicated the *time* of the different parts of the service.
4. ὡραΐζειν, because the deacon was beautified with it.
5. *Ora* (a coast), because (alleged to have been) originally the edging of a lost garment.
6. ὁράω, because the *sight* of it indicated whether a priest or deacon was ministering (!).

There can be little doubt that the first is the true etymology. The others are all more or less fanciful; and the *orarium* was certainly employed originally as a scarf. Ambrose speaks of the face of the dead Lazarus being bound with an *orarium*; and Augustine uses the same word to indicate a bandage employed to tie up a wounded eye.

Numerous effigies of late date are extant which exhibit a kind of scarf, passing over the left shoulder diagonally downwards to the right side, and fastened under the right arm. As Albertus Rubenius long ago pointed out, these scarves must not be confused with the *clavi* which ornamented the tunics of senators and *equites*; for they are worn over the *pallium*, or outer garment, and are disposed in a manner quite different from that in which the *clavi* fall.

What, then, are these scarves? The answer to this question is supplied by Flavius Vopiscus in his Life of Aurelian, who, he says, 'was the first to grant *oraria* to the Roman people, to be worn as favours.'* Now, the references which we have just made to Ambrose and Augustine — not to mention others which might equally well be quoted—show that the *oraria*, whatever may have been the method in which they were worn, must have been narrow strips of some kind of cloth. These peculiar scarves, which are to be seen on certain monuments, do not appear on any effigy dating before the time of Aurelian ; the natural inference, therefore, is that the scarves which we see thus represented are actually the *oraria*, granted to the Roman people by that emperor and his successors. If this argument be not valid, then it is impossible to say either what these scarves really are, or what was the true appearance of the civil *orarium*.

It is probable that considerable laxity existed in the manner of wearing the ecclesiastical *orarium*, for the fourth Council of Toledo thought it necessary to enact a special canon to regulate the method in which this vestment should be disposed. The fortieth act of this assembly restricts the number of *oraria* to one, and enjoins that deacons should wear the *orarium* over the left shoulder, leaving the right side free so as to facilitate the

* 'Sciendum ... illum ... primum donasse oraria populo Romano quibus uteretur populus ad favorem.'— Flav. Vop. in Aur., 48.

execution of their duties in Divine service.* This act also provides that the diaconal *orarium* should be plain, not ornamented with gold or embroidery. It will be noticed that this Toletan council favoured the derivation of the word *orarium* from *orare*.

The wearing of the *orarium* was still further regulated by two of the councils which met at Braga. The second council of Braga (563 A.D.) decreed that 'since in some churches of this province the deacons wear their *oraria* hidden under the tunic, so that they cannot be distinguished from the subdeacons, for the future they must be placed over their shoulders.'† The fourth

---

* 'Orariis duobus nec episcopo quidem licet nec presbytero uti; quanto magis diacono qui minister eorum est. Unum igitur orarium oportet Levitam gestare in sinistro humero propter quod orat, id est, praedicat; dextram autem partem oportet habere liberam ut expeditus ad ministerium sacerdotale discurrat. Caveat igitur amodo gemino uti orario sed uno tantum et puro nec ullis coloribus aut auro ornato.'— Acta Concil. Tolet. IV, cap. xl.

This rule does not seem to have been always obeyed. In the Pontifical of Landulfus (ninth century) there is a representation of an ecclesiastic wearing two *oraria*, one over each shoulder. This, however, must be regarded as exceptional.

† 'Item placuit ut quia in aliquantis huius provinciae ecclesiis diacones (*sic*) absconsis infra tunicam utuntur orariis ita ut nihil differre a subdiacono videantur de cetero superposito scapulae (sicut decet) utantur orario.'—Acta Concil. Bracar. II, cap. ix: Labbe, vol. v, col. 841. The eleventh

council (675 A.D.) made an important decree regulating the wearing of the *orarium* by priests, which has been since followed universally. The vestment was to be passed round the neck, over each shoulder, crossed in front, and secured in this position under the girdle of the *alba*.*

The last enactment of importance is that of the council of Mayence (813 A.D.), which ordered that priests should wear their *oraria* 'without intermission.'†

---

canon ordained 'ut lectores in ecclesia in habitu saeculari ornati non psallant.'

* 'Cum antiqua ecclesiastica noverimus institutione praefixum ut omnis sacerdos cum ordinatur orario utroque humero ambiatur; scilicet ut qui imperturbatus praecipitur consistere inter prospera et adversa, virtutum semper ornamento utrobique circumseptus appareat: qua ratione tempore sacrificii non assumat, quod se in sacramento accepisse non dubitatur? Proinde modis omnibus convenit ut quod quisque percepit in consecratione, hoc et retentet in oblatione, vel perceptione sude salutis; scilicet ut cum sacerdos ad sollennia missarum accedit aut pro se Deo sacrificium oblaturus, aut sacramentum corporis et sanguinis Domini Nostri Jesu Christi sumpturus, non aliter accedat, quam orario utroque humero circumseptus, sicut et tempore ordinationis suae dignoscitur consecraturus: ita ut de uno eodemque orario cervicem pariter et utrumque humerum premens, signum in suo pectore praeferat crucis. Si quis autem aliter egerit excommunicationi debitae subiacebit.'—Concil. Bracar. IV, cap. iv: Labbe, vol. vi, coll. 564, 565.

† 'Presbyteri sine intermissione utuntur orariis propter

The *orarium*, then, was a narrow strip of cloth, disposed about the persons of the clergy in various manners according to their rank. To it corresponded in name, shape, and method of disposition, a garment common among the Romans, though admittedly rather an honourable ornament than an actual article of clothing. Yet when we remember how the *clavi* were employed to distinguish rank among the earlier clergy, this latter fact may be regarded as strengthening the evidence of identity which the correspondence in all salient features affords. Some other theories of its origin will be discussed when we have treated of the *pallium*.

III. *The Planeta.* — In the earlier and purer days of the Roman people, the dress which alone was recognised as the proper costume for the citizen was the *toga*. This was one of the most inconvenient and cumbrous articles of dress ever invented—a great oblong cloth, fifteen feet by ten, thrown in a complicated manner over the left shoulder, folded in front, and hanging loose about the feet. We can hardly feel surprised at finding that, when the citizens came to regard comfort before appearances to such an extent as to adopt sleeved tunics, a more convenient form of this

---

differentiam sacerdotis dignitatis.'—Concil. Mogunt. cap. xxviii: Labbe, vol. vii, col. 1249.

outdoor costume was adopted. There were three varieties of this new* garment, each of which has its own name; these were the *paenula*, the *casula*, and the *planeta*.

The *paenula* was a garment which in the early days of the Republic was allotted to slaves. A slave wearing this dress is introduced into the 'Mostellaria' (IV iii 51) of Plautus. Indeed, according to Julius Pollux ('Onomasticon,' vii 61), the dramatist Rhinthon, who lived in the fourth century B.C., introduced a mention of this garment into his ' Iphigeneia in Tauris,' a fact which would seem to indicate that the dress was much older than his own time, as otherwise his audience would be unfavourably impressed by the anachronism. Numerous allusions in classical Latin authors show that it was adopted as a travelling dress because of its warmth and comparative convenience ;† but on no account was it worn within the walls of the city. Gradually, however, the use of the garment spread, till Alexander Severus (222-235 A.D.), as Lampridius tells us, permitted elders to wear the *paenula* within the city in cold

---

* Or, to speak more accurately, new adaptation of an old garment. The *paenula*, for instance, had long been worn by the lower classes, being cheap and warm.

† Though it was by no means adapted to active exertion. See Cicero, pro Milone, capp. x, xx.

weather, though at the same time he forbade women to do so except when on a journey.*

The *casula* was a poor and inferior variety of the *paenula*, which, when the latter was promoted to be the costume of senators and emperors, succeeded it as the garb of the poorer classes. The original meaning of the name is 'little house'— a diminutive of *casa*—and there is little evidence to guide us as to the exact appearance of the garment which it denoted. The name would lead us to infer that, like the *paenula*, it enveloped the entire body; but it is probable that it was made of coarser and cheaper material. The fact that it was early adopted as the distinctive dress of monks would lead us to this conclusion; beyond this there is no reason for supposing that it differed in outline from the *paenula*.

The *planeta* first appears in the fifth century A.D. Cassianus (De Habitu Monachorum, i 7) mentions it as a dress whose price prevents its use as a monastic habit; and St Isidore, two centuries later, expressly forbids members of religious orders to wear it. The *planeta* must therefore have been more costly than the *casula*, and, as we find it mentioned in the sixth century as the dress of

* 'Paenulis intra urbem frigoris causa ut senes uterentur permisit, quum id vestimenti genus semper itineranum fuisset aut pluviae. Matrones tamen intra urbem paenulis uti vetuit, in itinere permisit.'—Lamprid. in Alex. Sev., cap. xxvii.

The Early Development of Vestments. 45

nobles and of senators, it was probably the most expensive of the three.

The general shape of the garment, as shown in Roman paintings or effigies, is that of a cloak enveloping the body, sewn in front, and put on by being passed over the head, for which a suitable aperture was provided. And this shape is identical with the outer vestment which we see in early representations of clerics. The modification which was early adopted, that of making the vestment oval in form, so as to lessen the width over the shoulders and so to give more freedom to the arms, was obviously regulated by convenience.

Thus we have seen that the three principal vestments, as we find them detailed in the earliest lists and depicted in the earliest monuments, are identical in shape, disposition, and name with the Roman civil costume of the second or third century of the Christian era.

Three additional vestments are found enumerated in the letters of St Gregory the Great and elsewhere which were not worn universally throughout the church, but were either carefully confined to the clergy of the city of Rome itself or were in the gift, so to speak, of the Pope. These are the *pallium*, the *mappula*, and the *dalmatica*.

I. *The Pallium.*—In classical Latin this word is used either as the equivalent of *toga* or in the general sense of the English 'robe.' It is also

46 Ecclesiastical Vestments.

used in the earlier ecclesiastical writers of the *casula*, or coarse outer garment of monks, as in the passage from Celestine quoted on p. 26. Yet another use

FIG. 3.—ECCLESIASTICS FROM THE MOSAICS IN S VITALE, RAVENNA (SIXTH CENTURY).

of the word *pallium* is found in the expression *pallium linostimum*, which denoted a cloth, the use of which was ordained to deacons by Pope

The Early Development of Vestments. 47

Sylvester, as we shall presently see when discussing the maniple.

The *pallium*, when used by ecclesiastical writers in its proper and restricted sense, denotes an ornament specially appropriated to archbishops. Its earliest form is shown in the Ravenna mosaics—that of a narrow strip of cloth, passed over the left shoulder, looped loosely round the neck, and then passed over the left shoulder again, so that the two ends hang free, one in front, the other behind. This method of disposition seems to indicate an identity of origin with the *orarium*; indeed, it is sometimes difficult to distinguish between these vestments in early representations. A desire for symmetry, probably, decided the next step in its evolution; this consisted in bringing the free end to the middle and knotting it into the lowest point of the loop: this we find exemplified in monuments of the eighth, ninth, or tenth century. From this the transition to the form which became universal in later times was easy, and the two are found contemporaneously. The final form—which will be more fully described in the third chapter—is that of an oval loop with a long tail pendent from its ends, so that when the ornament is in position it presents the appearance of a capital Y on the front and on the back.

The early history of this vestment is involved

in deep obscurity. As already hinted, it is not improbably a modification of the *orarium*; but there is no evidence, further than general outward resemblance, that this is actually the case; nor is there any apparent reason for its appropriation to archbishops. The question must remain open till further research either reveals the missing links in the chain of connection, or elicits some more satisfactory solution of the question.

The idea of Dr Rock, according to which the *pallium* is viewed as 'the true and only representation of the Roman toga,' is most unsatisfactory. He thinks that the toga, which was folded over the left shoulder, under the right arm, over the right shoulder, and again over the left shoulder, 'dwindled down to a mere broad band,' folded much the same way; and that this broad band was the early *pallium*. The evolution here supposed is, however, most unnatural; there is not time for it to have taken place between the institution of Christianity and the date of the Ravenna mosaics—much less between the time when ecclesiastical vestments and their development began to receive special attention and the latter date; the toga, as we have already seen, was itself practically obsolete when Christianity began to make itself felt, and still further removed from the current fashion of the time at which archbishops began to require distinguishing in-

The Early Development of Vestments. 49

signia; and, lastly, the connecting links between the blanket at one end and the narrow strip of cloth at the other, which Dr Rock adduces and figures, are too few in number to be convincing, and quite explicable on other grounds, such as the unskilfulness of the ancient artist—a fruitful source of error in archæological research.

FIG. 4.—EFFIGY OF A ROMAN CITIZEN IN CAERLEON MUSEUM.

It is not inconceivable that the origin of the honourable *pallium* is to be sought in the honourable *orarium*, distributed as 'favours' to the Roman people; in which case we must seek elsewhere for a prototype to the ecclesiastical *orarium*. We should then fall back on the old idea, which has by no means been disproved, that in the *clavi* of the *tunica alba* is to be found the true original. We reproduce here a figure of an effigy of a Roman citizen at Caerleon, near Newport, which certainly seems to warrant this view; here is to be seen a *tunica*, a *clavus*, and a *paenula*, all very suggestive of the alb, stole, and chasuble of later times. Duchesne, in his 'Origines du culte chrétien,'* regards all the *orarium*-like vestments which appear in contemporary documents as in reality *pallia;* the *orarium* proper he does not consider to have been introduced till the tenth century. The *orarium* which appears before this date he regards as simply a napkin, or *sudarium*, designed to protect the *alba*. He further states that in the fourth century the civil law required all officials to wear some distinctive badge of office; that the Eastern Church complied with this law throughout, assigning the ὠμοφόριον, ἐπιτραχήλιον, and ὠράριον respectively to bishop, priest, and deacon, while the Western Church only complied with it to the extent of assigning a *pallium* to the bishops. We confess that this elaborate argument does not appeal to us any more than the theory which regards the stole as the orphrey of a degenerated vestment; but while professing our own belief in Marriott's view, stated above (pp. 38-9), we have given these several theories, leaving it to the reader to make his own choice.

From the earliest references to the *pallium* which we can find, it is clear that it was from the first regarded as a distinctive vestment to be worn

* Quoted by the Rev O. J. Reichel in his 'English Liturgical Vestments in the Thirteenth Century' (London, Hodges, 1895).

The Early Development of Vestments. 51

by archbishops only.* The archbishops of this early period had not the right, any more than their mediaeval successors, of assuming the *pallium* on their consecration; it was necessary to apply to the Pope for a grant of the vestment, which was only bestowed on the permission of the reigning sovereign being obtained. The earliest document unquestionably relating to the bestowal of the *pallium* is a letter of Pope Symmachus, bestowing the pallium on Theodore, Archbishop of Laureacus, in Pannonia, 514 A.D.† Instances of the royal assent being considered necessary are found in the letters of Pope Vigilius, who delayed the grant of the *pallium* to Archbishop Auxanius of Arles for two years, *pending the consent* of Childebert I, King of the Franks;‡ and in the letters of Pope Gregory the Great, who *at the request* of Childebert II bestowed the *pallium* on Virgilius, a later Archbishop of the same province.§

In 866 Pope Nicholas I declared that no archbishop might be enthroned or might consecrate the Eucharist till he should receive the *pallium* at the hands of the Pope.‖

* Some exceptions to this rule will be noticed in the next chapter.
† Symmachi Ep. xii in 'Patrologia,' lxii 72.
‡ Vigilii Epp. vi, vii in 'Patrologia,' lxix 26, 27.
§ Gregorii Ep. v 53; 'Patrologia,' lxvii 783.
‖ '.... sane interim in throno non sedentem et praeter corpus Christi non consecrantem priusquam pallium a sede

II. *The Mappula.*—We have seen in discussing the *alba* that Pope Sylvester, in the middle of the third century, decreed that the deacons of the city of Rome should substitute *dalmaticae* for *colobia;* he further charged them to wear a *pallium linostimum* on their hands. It is clear that this cloth, as its proper name, *mappula* (little napkin), demonstrates, was designed to serve the utilitarian purpose of a handkerchief, either to wipe the Communion vessels or the face of the minister — probably the latter.* This cloth, however, must early have become regarded as a sacred vestment by its wearers, and the exclusive privilege of the Roman priests to wear it was jealously guarded. Attempts were made by the deacons of the neighbouring churches of Ravenna to assume the vestment, and St Gregory found it necessary to interfere, which he did in

---

Romana percipiat, sicuti Galliarum omnes et Germaniae et aliarum regionum Archiepiscopi agere comprobantur.'— Nich. Papae I, Responsa ad consulta Bulgar., cap. lxxiii, *ad fin.*: Labbe, vol. viii, col. 542.

* The notion prevalent nowadays, that the *mappula* was exclusively intended to cleanse the sacred vessels, is thus bluntly negatived by St. Ivo of Chartres : 'Unde in sinistra manu ponitur quaedam mappula quae saepe fluentem oculorum pituitam tergat et oculorum lippitridinem removeat.' And Amalarius of Metz testifies to the same effect: 'Sudarium ad hoc portamus ut eo detergamus sudorem qui fit ex labore proprii corporis.'

several letters to that somewhat recalcitrant prelate, John, the Bishop of Ravenna. For the sake of peace, Gregory admitted a compromise whereby the principal deacons of Ravenna were allowed to wear the coveted ornament ; but the glamour of carrying a vestment, however inconvenient,* which was theoretically confined to the holy city itself, proved too strong a temptation for the deacons of other places, while the Romans (whose exclusive privilege was gone once Ravenna was admitted to a share in it) took no further steps to prevent its assumption. As a natural consequence, the use of the vestment spread over the whole of the Western Church, and by the time when the period at present engaging our attention ended, had become universal.

III. *The Dalmatica.*—We have already entered at length into the history of this word and of the vestment to which it was applied. It does not seem to have differed essentially from the *alba;* but it appears that two† vestments were worn at Rome, an *alba* and a *dalmatica*, though it is evident from the Toletan canons and other sources that at this early period such was not the case elsewhere. In early pictures the two vestments

---

* The modifications which the discomfort of this little vestment necessitated will be described in the next chapter.

† Civil dress presented parallel cases : the Emperor Augustus wore four tunics in cold weather.

are rarely represented side by side ; it is probable that the *dalmatica* was so long as to conceal the *alba*, just as the dalmatic on mediaeval effigies of Bishops often hides the tunicle. It seems, however, to have been shown on the ancient picture of Gregory the Great, described by Joannes Diaconus ; and we find that Gregory granted its use to Bishop Aregius of Gap and to his Archdeacon (Ep. ix 107 : Migne, lxxvii 1033), forwarding the vestments at the same time as the letter. Clearly the Pope does not denote the *alba* by the word *dalmatica*, as we have seen St Isidore of Seville do, for Aregius would naturally wear an *alba* without papal interference. The vestment in question must, therefore, have been another, resembling the alb in outline, but only worn either at Rome or by those on whom the Pope saw fit to confer it.

The history of the spread of the *dalmatica* must have been similar to that of the *mappula*. By the time the third period begins we find it established as an independent vestment, differing from its parent, the *alba*, in one important respect, which will be detailed in the following chapter.

Although not *vestments* in the strictest sense of the word, we must not conclude this chapter without a brief notice of the two exclusively episcopal insignia noticed in the canons of the fourth council of Toledo, namely, the ring and staff. Rings have been found in the tombs of bishops of the third century. This, however, proves nothing, as their use was universal among both Christians and heathen. Nor can anything definitely ecclesiastical be tortured out of the many descriptive notices which have come down to us of the rings in the possession of individual bishops of the third, fourth, and fifth centuries. Isidore of Seville (*circa* 600) lands us on firmer ground; he distinctly says : ' To the bishop at his consecration is given a staff . . . a ring likewise is given him to signify pontifical honour, or as a seal for secret things.'* We need not, perhaps, discuss the esoteric meaning of the gift as here set forth; but the fact clearly remains that by Isidore's time the gift of a ring and a staff had become an essential part of the ceremony of episcopal ordination. The Toletan canon tells us the same thing. Before that time there is no clear indication of the gift; it is not mentioned in ordination services of earlier date than the sixth century, one of the oldest references to it being in the sacramentary of Gregory the Great (*circa* 590 A.D.); and even this passage is rejected as an interpolation by Migne.†

* Huic dum consecratur datur baculus .... datur et annulus propter signum pontificalis honoris vel signaculum secretorum.—Isidorus de Off. Eccl., lib. ii, cap. v.

† *Ad annulum digito imponendam:* Accipe annulum fidei,

The Pastoral Staff.—Isidore says, in the passage already quoted, that the staff is given 'that he may rule or correct those set under him, or support the weakness of the weak.'[*]

It is strange that even the pastoral staff has a prototype among the insignia of the heathen priesthood. One of the emblems of the Roman augurs was a *lituus*, or crook, resembling almost exactly the earliest pastoral staves as we find them shown in the monuments of early Christian art. It was used *inter alia* for dividing the sky into regions for astrological purposes. The pastoral staff, as represented in early monuments, was much shorter than the mediaeval crozier; and it seems not at all improbable that the pastoral staff was originally a 'Christianization' of this pagan implement.

Other writers have argued in favour of the pastoral staff being simply an adaptation of the common walking-sticks, which were certainly used in churches as a support before the introduction of seats. It has been pointed out, however, that the pastoral staff had become a special member of the insignia of a bishop before the general abolition of these crutches; and this, it must be confessed, is

---

scilicet signaculum quatenus sponsam Dei, videlicet sanctam ecclesiam, intemerata fide ornatus illibate custodias.

[*] Ut subditam plebem vel regat vel corrigat vel infirmitatem infirmorum sustineat.

The Early Development of Vestments. 57

an argument of considerable force against such a hypothesis.

The letter of Celestine to the Bishops of Narbonne and Vienne, part of which we quoted on pp. 26-7, is probably about the earliest available reference to the use of the pastoral staff by members of the episcopal order. This brings the history of pastoral staves back to the early part of the fifth century, and shows that this special ornament was one of the earliest of the external symbols which the church has prescribed for its officers.

The staff was a rod of wood with a head either crutched or crooked, usually of one of the precious metals. The name suggests that the symbolism of the shepherd had entered largely into the ideas connected with it. It was carried by abbots and abbesses, by bishops, and, till about the tenth century, by the Pope; but with the rapid growth of the temporal sovereignty of the Papacy, the emblem purely associated with the special idea of spiritual pastorate was abandoned. In the old pre-scientific days it used to be stated that the Pope at no time carried

FIG. 5.—POPE GREGORY THE GREAT WITH PASTORAL STAFF.

a pastoral staff, though he did bear a *ferula*, or straight sceptre—the symbol of rule ;* but this is at variance with the evidence of contemporary art.

We must not leave the subject of the earliest form of ecclesiastical vestments without briefly noticing the ornamentation with which they were decorated. In the oldest representations of ecclesiastics which we possess, their vestments were represented pure white, ornamented with the *clavi* ; these were generally black, though St Isidore refers to purple *clavi*. But other colours appear in very early frescoes and mosaics. These, however, are apparently arbitrary, the result of the notions of the painter on the subject of the artistic combination of colours. Nothing analogous to the 'liturgical colours' of late times is traceable in the early or transitional period of the history of vestments.

Some ornamentation other than the *clavi* is found in vestments of late date in the present period. Leo III, the date of whose Papal rule lies just on the border-line between the transitional and the mediaeval epoch, presented to the Church of St Susanna a vestment with four *gam-*

* Romanus autem Pontifex Pastorali virga non utitur— Innoc. III Papa, De Sacr. Altar. Myst. i 62 (Migne ccxvii, 795). Ideoque summum Pontificem eiusmodi, incurvatam virgam non gerere quia eius potestas nullis locorum limitibus circumscribitur at ubique patet.—De Saussay, Panoplia Clericorum (Paris 1646), p. 102.

The Early Development of Vestments. 59

madia — that is, ornaments shaped like crosses formed by four gammas placed back to back, thus: ⌐⌐; we also hear of *calliculae*, metal or embroidered ornaments, for the *alba*. A singular method of ornamentation is exemplified by numerous frescoes and mosaics, and has been a fruitful source of perplexity to ecclesiologists. This consists in the use of letters (sometimes of monograms or letter-like arbitrary signs) on the outer hem of the garment. No connection can be traced between these letters and any circumstances known concerning the persons whose vestments they decorate ; and wide differences between the times and places of individual examples of the same character preclude their explanation as the faithful copies of weavers' marks. We can only say that their use is inexplicable on such practical or esoteric grounds, and that, therefore, some simple explanation, such as the arbitrary selection of a letter as an elementary ornament, is the only satisfactory means of accounting for their presence. Even now we daily employ rows of O-shaped circles, S-shaped curves, etc., as ornaments, without the slightest reference to the sounds which those symbols denote. The tendency to exalt simple little contrivances into hidden mysteries is ever with us, especially in ecclesiology, and it should on all occasions be repressed.

CHAPTER III.

THE FINAL FORM OF VESTMENTS IN THE WESTERN CHURCH.

HITHERTO, to a great extent, we have been groping in the dark, guided only by the dim light yielded by obscure passages in early writers or by half-defaced frescoes and shattered sculptures. Much is conjectural, much uncertain ; and often the shreds of information obtained from different sources appear contradictory, requiring patient thought and investigation to unravel the entanglement and reconcile the inconsistencies.

The progress of Christian literature and art had been retarded first by persecution, then by war and tumult. This partly accounts for the comparative scantiness of the material extant for a history of the Christian antiquities of the first eight centuries. But with the ninth century a new era began, which lasted unchecked all through the Middle Ages. The military genius of Charles the Great effected a general peace in the year 812; and under his enthusiastic patronage a true renaissance took place in learning and in art. Architecture and manuscript illumination were carried to a high degree of perfection, and for the first time active and systematic researches were made into the details of the doctrine and ritual of the church in the preceding centuries.

As a natural consequence of the inquiring spirit which thus made itself felt, the number of books and tracts on ecclesiastical matters multiplied enormously. Among the many branches of study which were and are open to the inquiry of the ecclesiologist, few occupied the attention of these ninth-century writers more than the vestments worn by the priests when ministering in Divine service.

It has been reserved for the antiquaries of our own day to formulate the true principles of scientific archaeology. We smile at the childish fancies which are gravely put forward in works not more than fifty years old; small wonder is it, then, that we find these early treatises on vestments disappointing. All are firmly impressed with the Levitical origin of the usage and shape of Christian vesture; and the majority are occupied with vague speculations concerning the symbolic meaning of the individual items in an ecclesiastical outfit.

Mr. Marriott assigns a reason for the then universal belief in the Levitical origin of ecclesiastical vestments which is highly ingenious, and probably correct. I cannot do better than cite his words on the subject:

'Churchmen who had travelled widely, as then some did, in East as well as West, could hardly fail to notice the remarkable fact, that at Constantinople as at Rome, at Canterbury as at Arles, Vienna or Lyons, one general type of ministering dress was maintained, varying only in some minor details; and that this dress everywhere presented a most marked contrast to what was *in their time* the prevailing dress of the laity. And as all knowledge of classical antiquity had for three centuries or more been well-nigh extinct in the church, it was not less natural that they should have sought a solution of the phenomenon thus presented to them in a theory of Levitical origin, which from that time forward was generally accepted.'*

Rabanus Maurus, as we have already stated (*supra*, p. 12), was the first who endeavoured to draw the parallel between the Christian and the Jewish vestments. The older writers saw the

* Vest. Christ., p. lxxviii.

difficulties in the way of establishing a complete correspondence. Thus Walfrid Strabo (*circa* 840), in chapter xxiv of his 'De Rebus Ecclesiasticis,' merely says: '*Numero autem suo antiquis respondent*' (In their *number* they correspond to the ancient vestments); and he further admits that mass was formerly celebrated by a priest robed in everyday dress.* But, as the desire to prove the correspondence grew more widespread, changes and additions were rapidly made in the vestments themselves, with a view to assimilating the two systems. In the interval between the ninth and eleventh centuries the number of recognised vestments was doubled by the accretions thus made to the original set.

As the simplest and most intelligible method of exhibiting the extent of these changes, I have drawn up the subjoined table, in which are given the lists of vestments known to writers on ecclesiastical matters during this interval of time. These lists are placed in parallel columns, and a uniform system of nomenclature has been adopted, so that the reader can see at a glance the date of the various additions:

* Vestes etiam sacerdotales per incrementa ad eum qui nunc habetur auctae sunt ornatum. Nam primis temporibus communi indumento vestiti missas agebant, sicut et hactenus quidam Orientalium facere perhibentur.—Walafrid Strabo De Reb. Eccl., cap. xxiv (Migne cxiv 952).

Rabanus Maurus, circa 820.	Pseudo-Alcuin, saec. x.	Ivo of Chartres, ob. 1115.	Honorius of Autun, circa 1130.	Innocent III, circa 1200.
Alb	Alb	Alb	Alb	Alb
Girdle	Girdle	Girdle	Girdle	Girdle
Amice	Amice	Amice	Amice	Amice
Stole	Stole	Stole	Stole	Stole
Maniple	Maniple	Maniple	Maniple	Maniple
Dalmatic	Dalmatic	Dalmatic	Dalmatic	Dalmatic
Chasuble	Chasuble	Chasuble	Chasuble	Chasuble
Sandals	Sandals	Sandals	Sandals	Sandals
Pall	Pall	...	Pall	Pall
...	...	Stockings	...	Stockings
...	...	...	Subcingulum	Subcingulum
...	...	...	Rational	...
...	...	...	Mitre	Mitre
...	...	...	Gloves	Gloves
...	...	...	Ring	Ring
...	...	...	Staff	Staff
...	...	...	...	Tunicle
...	...	...	...	Orale

From this table it will be seen that the number of vestments was increased, not so much by the invention of entirely new ornaments, as in the exaltation to the rank of separate 'vestments' of what had previously been subordinate. The ring and staff, for instance, were known to the councillors at Toledo, but they do not appear in these lists till the twelfth century.

We must now discuss each of these vestments, noting their shape and the peculiarities which they presented at different times. It will be convenient to follow the order of the above table.

The Final Form of Vestments. 65

I. *The Alb.*—We have traced the history of this vestment from its use as a purely secular garment till the ninth century, and have seen how its proportions, at first ample, were contracted till the vestment fitted with comparative tightness to the body, on account of the greater convenience which the less flowing form of the vestment offered for active administration in Divine service.

The material of which the alb was made was usually linen, of more or less fine quality; but we often meet with entries in old inventories of church goods which enumerate albs of other material. Silk and cloth of gold are very commonly mentioned, and velvet is not unknown. Thus we have

'Albe sunt viginti de serico principales.'—Inv. Westminster Abbey, 1388.

'30 albes of old cloth of Baudkyn.'—Inv. Peterborough, 1539.

'One olde aulbe of whyte velvyt.'—Inv. St Martin Dover, 1536.

The proper colour of the alb was white; but in England coloured albs were sometimes worn, and we meet with such vestments in inventories *passim*. The following is a selection :

'Red albes for Passion week, 27.
'40 Blue albes of divers sorts.
'7 Albes called Ferial black.'—Inv. Peterborough, 1539.
'Alba de rubea sindone brudata.'—Inv. Canterbury.

The ornamentation of the alb, in the earlier

5

years of the third period, sometimes consisted of round gold plates, just above the lower hem of the vestment, one on either side. Occasionally there were rows of small gold plates arranged round the lower edge. Albs of the first kind were called *albae sigillatae*, from the seal-like appearance of the gold plates. Albs of the second kind were named *albae bullatae*. Dr Rock quotes the following :

'Camisias albas sigillatas holosericas.'—Record of gift of King Æthelwulf to St Peter's, Rome, in Liber Pontific. in Vita Benedicti III, t. iii, p. 168, ed. Vignolio.

'Alba bona et bullata.'—Peterborough, A.D. 1189.

The more usual ornamentation, however, and that which became universal in later years, consisted in ornamental patches of embroidery, technically called *apparels*, sewn on to various parts of the vestment. There were two such rectangular patches just above the lower hem,* one in front, one behind ; two similar patches, one on the back, the other on the breast ; two small patches, one on each cuff; a narrow strip encircling the aperture for the head, more for use (as a binding to prevent tearing) than for ornament ; and, in earlier examples, two narrow strips running down in

* Very often—perhaps more often than not—the lower hem was ornamented with a narrow edging of embroidery running all round. In some albs as represented on Continental monuments there is a considerable distance between the apparel and the hem.

front and two behind, like the *clavi* of the Roman tunic.

In the earliest representations of albs, as seen on sculptured monuments, the vestment is left plain; one of the earliest apparelled albs being on an effigy to the memory of Bishop Giffard, at Worcester, 1301. This, however, does not imply more than that the apparels were originally painted on, and that the paint has worn off.

Another difference is observable between the cuff-apparels of early effigies and of those of later date. In the early albs the cuff-apparel invariably encircles the whole wrist; but in later specimens we find that it has shrunk to a small square patch, sewn on the part of the sleeve which is toward the back of the hand.

Dr Rock has shown some reason for believing that the apparels were occasionally hung loose over their proper place; the lower hem apparels being suspended from the girdle, and those on the breast and back being fastened together by two cords, between which the head was passed, and which consequently, when in position, ran across the shoulders. This was obviously suggested by convenience; for the entry in the accounts of St Peter's, Sandwich—

'for washing of an awbe and an amyce parteÿing to the vestments of the garters and flour de lice and for sewing on of the parelles of the same, v^d'

—tells us what we should have expected, that the apparels had to be removed from the vestment when it was washed, and sewn on again afterwards. It was only natural that some such plan as the loose suspension of the apparels should be followed; for the constant ripping off and sewing on of the embroidery must have been not only laborious, but ultimately detrimental to the vestment.

This entry gives us an instance of another fact, that vestments and suits of vestments were named after the pattern which was embroidered upon their apparels. A singular collection occurs in the Peterborough inventory, including

> '6 albes with Peter keys.
> '6 albes called the Kydds.
> '7 albes called Meltons.
> '6 albes called Doggs.'

Albs were sometimes worn plain, *i.e.*, without apparel. The Salisbury Missal, for example, forbids the apparelled alb to be worn on Good Friday; and it is not at all impossible that some of the plain albs, as represented on early monuments, are really intended for unadorned vestments.

Some difference of opinion seems to exist among the authorities about the mystical signification of this vestment. Rabanus Maurus holds it to inculcate purity of life. Amalarius of Metz, contrasting Jerome's description of the tight-fitting

Jewish tunic with the flowing alb of his own day, considers that it denotes the liberty of the New Testament dispensation as contrasted with the servitude of the Old. Pseudo-Alcuin thinks that it means perseverance in good deeds, and that therefore Joseph is described as wearing a *tunica talaris* among his brethren. 'For a tunic which reaches all the way to the ankles is a good work carried out to the end, for the ankle is the end of the body.' Ivo of Chartres asserts that it signifies the mortification and chastisement of the members. Honorius of Autun agrees more or less with Rabanus Maurus; but Innocent III regards it as symbolical of newness of life, 'because it is as unlike as possible to the garments of skins which are made from dead animals, and with which Adam was clothed after his fall.'

The following dimensions are among those given by Mrs Dolby as the correct measurements of an alb for a figure of medium height and ordinary proportions:

	ft.	in.
Length behind when made	4	9
Length before	4	5
Depth of shoulder-band	0	$8\frac{1}{2}$
Width of same	0	$1\frac{1}{4}$
Length of sleeve, outside of arm	2	$1\frac{1}{2}$
Width of sleeve at wrist folded in two	0	$6\frac{1}{2}$
Width of sleeve half-way up	0	$9\frac{1}{2}$
Length of neck-band	2	$2\frac{1}{4}$
Width of same	0	$1\frac{1}{4}$
Opening down front	1	$1\frac{1}{2}$

II. *The Girdle*, with which the alb is secured, is a narrow band, usually of silk, the ends of which terminate in a tassel.

The colour of the girdle is properly white, though occasionally it varied with the colour of the day. Though (as stated) properly of silk, it is sometimes made of cotton.

Occasionally the girdle was embroidered in colours. In the Westminster inventory of 1388 we have:

'Zone serice sunt septem diversi operis et diversorum colorum.'

The following is a selection of the esoteric meanings ascribed to this vestment: *custodia mentis; discretio omnium virtutum; virtus continentiae; perfecta Christi caritas.*

The length of the girdle is stated at about four yards. The length of the alb, it should be noticed, was so considerable that it was necessary to draw it through the girdle and let it hang over above it. It is therefore extremely rare (if not unknown) for the girdle to be visible on mediaeval monuments, for even in those exceptional effigies in which the whole length of the alb is visible, the latter vestment entirely conceals the girdle by falling over it.

III. *The Amice.*—This vestment was quite unknown in the earlier period : it was a mediaeval invention.

The Final Form of Vestments. 71

The amice was clearly originally intended to serve as a hood; and a survival of this use remains in the ritual of vesting, in which the priest first places the vestment on his head, with the prayer 'Impone Domine capiti meo galeam salutis ad expugnandum diabolicos incursus,' before adjusting it round his neck.

In several dioceses of France the amice was worn as a hood upon the head from All Saints' Day till Easter, and something of the same kind may have been the practice elsewhere; thus, we find an effigy of a priest in Towyn, Merionethshire, and another in Beverley Minster, in which the amice is drawn over the head hoodwise.

In shape the amice was a rectangle (the dimensions are given as thirty-six inches by twenty-five inches). At each end strings were sewn, which were of sufficient length to cross over the breast and encircle the body. An apparel of embroidered work ran along one of the long sides; so that when the vestment was in position it was turned down, like a collar, over the other vestments round the neck, and so far open as to leave the throat of the wearer exposed. A small cross was marked in the centre of the upper edge of the vestment.

So much of this vestment was concealed that there appears to have been little or no scope for variety of treatment, either in form or material. The latter seems always to have been linen. The *orphreys* (embroidered edges), of course, are subject to the same unlimited variation of design as the corresponding ornaments on other vestments; but the shape is constant.

The same uniformity is not, however, observable in the symbolism of this vestment. The variety of meanings is even greater than is the case with the alb and its girdle. We are told that it signifies (*inter alia*) the Holy Incarnation; the purity of good works; the subjugation of the tongue; the earthy origin and heavenly goal of the human body; the necessity of justice and mercy in addition to temperance and abstention from evil; and the endurance of present hardships.

IV. *The Stole.*—The early history of the stole has been discussed in the preceding chapter, in considering the *orarium*.

Why, or when, the proper name of the vestment became 'stole,' or *stola*, does not appear. It is named *stola* in the later ecclesiastical canons of our second period; but it is not clear how *stola*, which in its original significance denoted a flowing tunic, like the under-garment of the Roman or the *alba* of the priests of the second period, came to signify a narrow strip of orphreywork. It is quite certain that it cannot be explained (as some writers have attempted to do) as the *orphrey* of a lost vestment which has survived while the bulk of it has disappeared; for

The Final Form of Vestments. 73

the continuity of the stole and the *orarium* is a matter of historic certainty, and we have already shown reason for assigning an entirely different origin to the latter vestment. Such an evolution, too, as that of a narrow strip from a large vestment is not natural, and is contrary to our observation in the history of other vestments; and it assumes the existence of embroidered 'orphreys' at a time far too remote for such ornamentation

FIG. 6.—STOLE-ENDS, SHOWING VARIETIES IN FORM AND ORNAMENT.

to be found. This hypothesis has suggested one of the less probable etymologies which have been proposed for the word *orarium*.

The stole is a narrow strip of embroidered work, nine or ten feet long and two or three inches wide. In its original form it was of the same width throughout; but about the thirteenth or fourteenth century we find its ends terminating in a rectangular compartment, giving each the appearance of a tau cross. This was in order to secure extra room for the cross with which every stole was supposed to be marked at the end. For the same purpose the modern stole expands gradually from the middle point, where also a cross is embroidered.

Priests wear the stole between the alb and chasuble, crossed over the breast, and secured in that position by the girdle of the alb—nowadays only when officiating at mass, formerly on all occasions on which the stole was worn. Deacons generally secure it over the left shoulder and under the right arm, thereby approximating the disposition of the vestment to that of the ancient Roman ornament from which the vestment takes its origin. Bishops wear the stole between the alb and tunicle* pendent perpendicularly on either side of the breast; the pectoral cross which they wear is supposed to supply the place of the crossed stole.

The embroidery and material of the stole were supposed to tally with that of the alb, with which it was worn. The same rule applies to the maniple, and we commonly find in inventories that the three vestments are catalogued together. But if we can trust the evidence of brasses and other monuments, the vestments of different suits were worn together in a very haphazard manner,

---

* The late brass of Bishop Goodrich, in Ely Cathedral, represents the stole between the tunicle and dalmatic. This is exceptional, and probably an engraver's error.

and it does not seem possible to extract any definite rule as to the collocation of different vestments embroidered with different patterns of orphreys.

The ends of the stole—below the embroidered cross when such existed—terminated in a fringe; and it was not uncommon in earlier years for little bells to be included in this fringe. Thus we have :

'Una stola cum frixio Anglicano cum perlis albis et endicis et campanellis.'—Inv. Vest. Papae Bonif. VIII, *cit. ap.* Rock, 'Church of our Fathers.'

The stole is said to signify 'the easy yoke of Christ.' Authorities earlier than the twelfth century are agreed on this point, though they differ on some minor details in the subordinate symbolism of its length, disposition, etc. But Honorius of Autun asserts that it signifies 'innocence,' and makes some vague and, to the present writer, unintelligible allusions to Esau's sale of his birthright; while Innocent III, with a faint reminiscence of the earlier exegesis, declares it to signify the servitude which Christ underwent for the salvation of mankind—referring to Phil. ii 5-8.

V. *The Maniple.*—The history of the development of the maniple follows closely on that of the stole. With a very few exceptions, the maniple, as represented on mediaeval monuments, differs from the stole, with which it is associated, in size alone.*

The maniple was originally worn over the fingers of the left hand. This arrangement was most inconvenient, as it was constantly liable to slip off, and the fingers had to be held in a con-

FIG. 7.—ARCHBISHOP STIGAND. (From the Bayeux tapestry, showing maniple carried over fingers.)

strained attitude throughout the service. It was early found more comfortable and convenient to place the vestment over the left wrist; but no

* One of these exceptions is presented by a small brass of a priest (Thomas Westeley, 1535) at Wyvenhoe, near Colchester.

The Final Form of Vestments. 77

definite rule seems to have been formulated, and, indeed, in some parts of France the earlier custom seems to have survived till the middle of the eighteenth century. When placed on the wrist it was either buttoned or sewn so as to form a permanent loop, so that it should not slip off the arm.

In a few effigies the maniple is represented on the right wrist. For this there is no liturgical authority, and it can only be attributed to the blundering of the engraver or sculptor.*

In reference to its original utilitarian purpose, Amalarius assigns to the maniple the significance of the 'purification of the mind.' Pseudo-Alcuin holds it to denote this present life (in qua superfluos humores patimur). It is also said to denote penitence, caution, and the prize in the racecourse.

The width of the maniple is the same as that of the stole—the length is given at from three feet to three feet eight inches.

* There is a remarkable statuette of alabaster in the Cambridge Museum of Archaeology, which originally formed part of a retable in Whittlesford Church, Cambridgeshire. In this figure, which is clad in Eucharistic vestments, the maniple is absent, and its place seems to be supplied by a *chain* suspended over the *right* wrist. This may, however, represent some such saint as St Leonard, whose emblem is a chain and manacles : in which case it is just possible that the sculptor omitted the maniple to avoid the inartistic symmetry which would result from its insertion.

VI. *The Dalmatic.*—I am unable to find any representation of this vestment older than the ninth century, showing the special features which distinguished it from the other vestments of the mediaeval period. Before that date the dalmatic

FIG. 8.—DEACON IN EPIS-COPAL DALMATIC. (From Randworth Church.)

FIG. 9.—DEACON IN DIACONAL DALMATIC.

seems to have been identical with the *alba*, possibly distinguished from it by being a little shorter when, as at Rome, the two vestments were worn together.

In the mediaeval period, however, this vestment (and its modification, the tunicle) is marked out from all others by being slit up a short distance on either side. These side-slits were decorated with fringes; but here an important theoretical distinction must be observed between the dalmatic of a bishop and that of a deacon. This was often neglected in mediaeval times, and is consequently frequently overlooked by ecclesiologists of the present day. In the dalmatic, as worn by a bishop, the side-slits, the lower hems, and the ends of the sleeves were fringed; in the dalmatic of a deacon there were also fringes, *but only on the left sleeve and along the left slit.*

The true reason for this distinction is probably to be sought in the same direction as that which prompted the peculiar diaconal method of wearing the *orarium*—convenience. The deacon, who was practically the servitor at the altar, required to have his right side free and unhampered as much as possible; the heavy fringes, which might have impeded him, were therefore dispensed with upon that side. But such an explanation would by no means satisfy the early mediaeval writers on vestments, and we are accordingly informed that as the left side typifies this present life and the right that which is to come, so the fringes on the left indicate those cares through which we must pass in this world, while their absence on the right symbolizes our freedom from care in the world to come. Why the bishop was not regarded as exempt from care in the future world does not appear.

Another singular piece of blundering meets us at St David's Cathedral. Here we have two effigies representing clerics, who, though they wear the dalmatic, yet show the stole disposed symmetrically, in the manner of priests.* Either the presence of the dalmatic or the presbyteral stole must be incorrect; but in our ignorance of the identity of the persons whom these effigies commemorate we cannot decide which. Bloxam's idea, that these figures represent archdeacons, though ingenious, is untenable; for there is no authority for assigning the dalmatic to an archdeacon of priestly grade; and we have other figures of priests known to have been archdeacons in various parts of England, none of which show the dalmatic.

The ornamentation of the dalmatic before the twelfth century consisted either of vertical bands (like the *clavi*) or else of horizontal bands, of orphrey-work. After that date the plain white vestment was superseded by one covered all over with elaborate embroidery. This is especially the case with the episcopal dalmatic, which is only what we should have expected.

We have already stated one symbolical meaning

* This description is given on the authority of Bloxam, companion volume, p. 64.

The Final Form of Vestments. 81

attaching to the dalmatic and its appurtenances. A few more may be of interest : the Passion of Christ ; the 'pure religion and undefiled,' as described by St James ; the Old and New Testaments ; the crucifixion of the world in the wearer ; the wide mercy of Christ, etc.

All of the early writers are misled by the decree of Pope Sylvester into imagining that Sylvester first instituted this garment as a purely ecclesiastical vestment ; some even go the length of assigning a mystical meaning to the *colobium*, which it superseded. Even Walafrid Strabo, who in many respects is the least mystical of the early mediaeval writers on ecclesiastical vestments, is deceived, though he wisely contents himself with stating the fact that Sylvester had so commanded, without attempting to assign any reason for his so doing.

VII. *The Chasuble.*—The variety of materials of which the chasuble was made may be gathered from the following extracts from the Lincoln Inventory of 1536 :

'Imprimis a Chesable of rede cloth of gold w‍ᵗ orfreys before and behind sett w‍ᵗ perles blew white and rede w‍ᵗ plaits of gold enamelled.'

'Item a Chesuble of Rede velvett w‍ᵗ kateryn wheils of gold.'

'Item a chesuble of Rede sylk browdered w‍ᵗ falcons & leopardes of gold.'

'Item a chesable of whyte damaske browdered wᵗ flowres of gold.'
'Item a chesable of whyte tartaroñ browdered wᵗ treyfoyles of gold.'
'Item a chesable of purpur satten lynyd wᵗ blew bukerham havyng dyverse scripturs.'
'Item a chesable of cloth of tyshew wᵗ orfreys of nedyll wark.'
'Item a chesable of sundon browdered wᵗ mones & sterres lyned wᵗ blew bukerham.'

Of the materials here mentioned the commonest were velvet, silk, or cloth of gold.

In the latest days of the transitional and the earliest days of the mediaeval period, there were two kinds of chasubles in use, the eucharistic and the processional. The distinction between them was utilitarian rather than ritualistic; it consisted in a hood sewn to the back of the latter, and designed as a covering for the head during outdoor processions in inclement weather. But the processional chasuble early gave place to the cope; and a hooded chasuble does not appear to be extant in representations of date later than the tenth century.

The manner in which the early chasubles were made seems to have been as follows: A semicircular piece of the cloth of which the vestment was to consist was taken, and a notch cut at the centre, so that the shape of the cloth resembled that of the figure in the annexed diagram; the

The Final Form of Vestments. 83

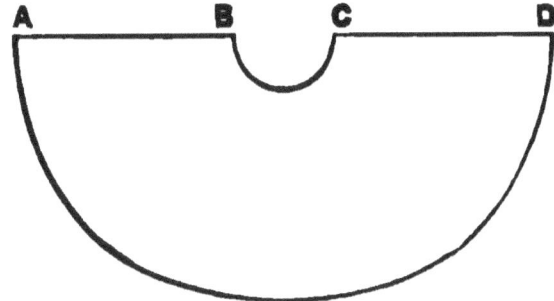

two straight edges corresponding to the lines AB and CD were then brought together and sewn; the result was a vestment somewhat of extinguisher shape, with a hole in the middle for the neck, and enveloping the body all round to an equal depth each way. The result was that when the priest had to raise his hands the vestment was gathered inconveniently on either shoulder, and probably injured by being crushed, certainly hampering the wearer by its weight. This difficulty was surmounted by a very simple expedient. The cloth, instead of being shaped as before, was cut into an oval form, and an opening was made at the centre for the wearer's head, the consequence being that when in position the vestment hung down over the front and back to some distance, and covered the upper part of the arms, though not sufficiently so to interfere with their free action. The latter shape is that which meets us all through the mediaeval period throughout the Western Church.

The modern Roman Church has made yet another innovation which, although it has its disadvantages, certainly reduces the inconvenience of the vestment to a minimum. Two fairly large semicircular pieces are cut from each side of the front of the vestment, thereby permitting the hands to be brought together when necessary without crushing the vestment between the forearms, which was inevitable in the old form. But the wasp-waisted appearance of this chasuble is ugly, and attempts are being made to abolish it and to return to the mediaeval pattern.

FIG. 10.—SIR PETER LEGH, KNIGHT AND PRIEST. (From his brass at Winwick. Vested in chasuble only.)

Yet another small distinction is to be found in the shape of individual examples of the mediaeval period. We find many of these vestments to be made circular or elliptical, so that the lower border is rounded off; while many others are found to be made in the shape known as the *vesica piscis*, so that the lower extremities terminate in a point more or less sharp. Writers who cannot be content with

The Final Form of Vestments. 85

simple or commonplace explanations of such phenomena as this have laboured in vain to invent some esoteric signification which will account for it. Perhaps the most common-sense guess is that made by Dr Rock, who thinks that the rounded chasuble was used during the period of rounded architecture—the Saxon and Norman —and the pointed chasuble during the pointed periods of architecture : a suggestion which we should have no difficulty in accepting at once, were it not for the fact that scores of brasses and other monuments of the Curvilinear and Rectilinear periods in architecture exist showing *rounded* chasubles ; while (among others) the effigy of Bishop John de Tour, at Bathampton near Bath, A.D. 1123, shows a *pointed* vestment. We have no space to enter into particulars of the other suggestions—the symbolism of the *vesica piscis*, the perfection of the circle, etc.

The simple explanation seems to be that the difference depended merely on the taste and fancy of the seamstress or of the engraver of the monument. It would be perfectly possible to draw up a list of monuments in which the point of the chasuble shows every stage from extreme sharpness to extreme bluntness, and so, by one step further, into a continuous curve. This demonstrates that no rule was necessarily followed in choosing the shape of the chasuble, beyond that of making a fairly symmetrical vestment which should hang down in front and behind, and should have a hole in the middle through which the priest's head should be passed. Nor can we even say that fashion affected the shape of the vestment; for were such a list as I have mentioned to be printed here, it would be seen to consist of the most haphazard and random series of dates and names of places thrown together without the slightest regard to chronological sequence or geographical position.

The dimensions of a pointed chasuble (*circa* fourteenth century) at Aix-la-Chapelle, which has been accepted as a standard for modern imitation, are given as follows:

	ft.	in.
Depth of shoulder, measuring from neck	2	9
Length of side, from shoulder to point	4	11
Depth from neck to point in front	4	6
,, ,, ,, behind	4	10

The chasuble of St Thomas of Canterbury, at Sens Cathedral, which is of the old extinguisher shape, is three feet ten inches in depth. In the oldest chasubles the length of the vestment behind was greater—often much greater—than in front. There is a more even balance between back and front in later mediaeval times.

Passing now from the manner of making the chasuble to the manner of ornamenting it, we find just the same divergence, with apparently just as

The Final Form of Vestments. 87

little rule. It is probable that, as the decoration was the most costly part of the manufacture of a chasuble, the amount of it was regulated by the resources available to pay for it.

We propose to consider at the end of the next chapter the classes of patterns with which vestments generally were decorated in the middle ages; at present, therefore, we shall confine ourselves to noticing briefly the positions in which these decorations were placed on the chasuble.

The groundwork of the vestment was either plain (invariably so in the older examples) or else embroidered or woven with a pattern, according to taste and means; the ornamentation proper consisted of strips of embroidered or 'orphrey' work, as it is technically called, sewn on to the vestment. These strips were sewn either on the edge or crosswise on the front and back of the chasuble.

The edge orphrey is the more frequently met with in the brasses of parish priests, and it is rarely so elaborately decorated as are the central orphreys. It usually consisted of some simple pattern of flowers or geometrical figures recurring at regular intervals round the edge.

Greater variety is seen in the shape of the central orphrey, which, being the more elaborate and expensive, is almost invariably found represented in the monuments of bishops, abbots, and other dignitaries, and in the effigies of priests of the richer churches. It sometimes, though rarely, consisted of a simple 'pillar' on front and on the back of the vestment; usually this ornamentation was extended by the addition of branches of orphrey work given off on either side, which passed over the shoulder and joined the corresponding branches of the other pillar, the result being that the orphrey on front and back had the appearance of the Greek Ψ, or of a Latin cross with oblique arms. When the bands were so disposed, the pillar on the front was called the *pectoral*, the pillar on the back the *dorsal*, and the auxiliary bands, which passed over the shoulders, the *humeral* orphreys. Very frequently this design was varied by omitting the part of the pectoral and dorsal bands above their intersection with the humeral; this resulted in the 'Y cross,' which we find in so many effigies in our cathedrals and churches. In a few examples the Y or Ψ is inverted, and in some it gives off auxiliary branches, so as to resemble (*e.g.*) the figure ✕. It would, however, be waste of time and space to enter further into a discussion of what was not regulated by any definite rule, but depended on caprice, or, at most, on pecuniary considerations. More often than not the central orphrey, of whatever form, is combined with the edge orphrey, and is usually of a different pattern from it.

In many early chasubles the front and back are

The Final Form of Vestments. 89

charged with an embroidered Latin cross. This is also the case with the back of the modern Roman or slit vestment.

When the Y orphrey was placed on the chasuble, the space between it and the neck on the back was usually filled with an elaborate floral design embroidered in gold or crimson. Sometimes (not always) this extended round the neck, and was repeated in front. To this ornament the special name of 'flower' has been attached.

The chasuble surmounts and safeguards all the other vestments; hence the chasuble signifies love, which surmounts all the other virtues, and safeguards and illumines their beauty with its protection; so says Rabanus Maurus, prettily enough. Amalarius disagrees; he holds that as the chasuble is common to all clerics, so it ought to set forth the works which are common to all: fasting, thirsting, watching, poverty, reading, singing, praying, and the rest. The pseudo-Alcuin and Ivo of Chartres agree with Rabanus, though for different reasons. Innocent III, however, holds it to signify the virtue of apostolical succession: 'For this is the vestment of Aaron, to the skirt of which the oil ran down; but it ran down from his head to his beard and from his beard to the skirt. Forasmuch as we all receive of His spirit, first the Apostles, afterwards the rest.' Further, he goes on to say that because the stretching out of the hands divides the chasuble into two complete and similar parts, so that vestment typifies the old and new church before and after the time of Christ.

VIII. *The Sandals.*—The sandals of the Roman citizens are well known — mere soles, secured across the instep by one or more thongs of leather, and clearly designed to protect the wearer from stony roads without unnecessarily cramping or confining his feet—an important consideration in a hot climate.

Such a sandal must have been worn by the early clergy as Roman citizens, and probably long continued in use among the lower orders of clerics. It was, and still is, the only foot-covering of certain monastic orders, and in some cases was retained even by monks who had attained to episcopal rank. In St Canice's Cathedral, Kilkenny, which contains a unique collection of mediaeval effigies and incised slabs, superior in merit to many better-known specimens of mediaeval art, there exists a most interesting effigy of a former bishop, de Ledrede, who died *circa* 1350. He is represented fully vested in Eucharistic dress; but in place of the episcopal sandals, which an ordinary bishop would have worn, he wears the simpler monastic sandal, which covers only the sole and instep; and shows the cord of St Francis hanging below his alb.

The Final Form of Vestments. 91

The extension of the Church into more northern and colder regions, and the importation of foreign customs into the southern metropolis itself, probably suggested the transformation of the somewhat scanty sandal into a more appropriate and more comfortable shoe. The traditions of the old custom were, however, long maintained in a curious way : the upper leathers of the shoe were fenestrated or cut into open-work patterns, the result being that the bare surface of the foot showed through and displayed the decoration in light flesh-tint against the dark leather of the shoe. When the episcopal stocking was added to the equipment of the bishop, the colour became bright scarlet, though the effect remained much the same.

The fenestrated sandals were abandoned about the fourteenth century in favour of shoes, in shape very much resembling the modern ankle-shoe. It would have been inconsistent, however, with the spirit of the fourteenth century to have abandoned the decorative effect produced by the open-work, and neglected to find some substitute. This substitute was found in lavish embroidery and in ornamentation with jewels and spangles of gold. The sandals, in fact, became as elaborate as did the rest of the ecclesiastical vestments.

The sandals, as above described, were worn by bishops only, at the Eucharistic service. Deacons and priests appear to have worn simple everyday shoes, without ornamentation of any kind. The fenestrated shoes (which were popular among the dandies of the day as well as consecrated to the bishops) were expressly forbidden to them, as also were coloured shoes, or shoes of the preposterous shapes occasionally in vogue among the laity of the middle ages.

'As the sandals partly cover the feet and leave them partly bare,' says Rabanus, 'so the teachers

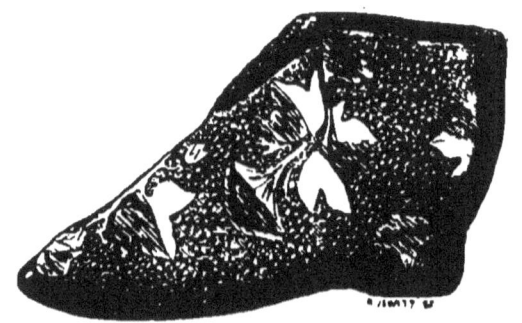

Fig. 11.—Bishop Waynflete's Episcopal Sandal.

of the Gospel should reveal part of the Gospel and should hide the rest, that the faithful and pious may have enough knowledge thereof, and the infidel and despiser may find no matter for blasphemy. And this kind of shoe warns us likewise that we should have a care to our flesh and our bodies in matters of necessity, not in matters of lust.'

Amalarius of Metz enters into further details, incidentally touching on some points of difference which obtained between the sandal of the bishop and that of the priest in his day—the first half of the ninth century. The following is a translation of his words:

'The difference in the sandal sets forth a difference in the minister. The offices of the priest and of the bishop are almost identical; but because there is a distinction in their titles and honours there is a distinction in their sandals, that we may not fall into error upon beholding them, which we might well do, owing to the similarity of their offices. The bishop has a band (*ligatura*) in his sandals, which the presbyter has not. It is the duty of the bishop to travel throughout the length and breadth of his diocese (*parochia*) to govern the inhabitants; and lest they should fall from his feet, his sandals are bound. The moral of this is, that he who mingles with the vulgar crowd must secure fast the courses of his mind (*gressus mentis*). The priest, who remains in one spot and offers the sacrifice there, walks more securely. The deacon, because his office is different from that of the bishop, needs not different sandals; he therefore wears them bound, because it is his to go on attendance. The subdeacon, because he assists the deacon, and has almost the same office, must have different sandals, that he be not thought a deacon. The inner meaning is this: Because the sandals set forth the way of the preacher, the sole, which is underneath, warns the preacher not to mingle with earthly matters. The tongue of white leather, which is under the " tread "* of the foot, shows that there ought to be the same separation, guiltless and guileless ; that it may be said of him, " Behold an Israelite indeed, in whom there is no guile ;" let him not be such as were the false apostles, who preached in malice and disputation. The tongue, which rises thence, and is separated from the leather of the sandals, sets forth the tongue of those who ought to bear good testimony to the preacher, of whom Paul said, " He must have a good report of them that are without." These are in the lower rank, and to some extent are separated from spiritual intercourse. The upper tongue is the tongue of the spirits (*spiritalium*), who lead the preacher into the work of preaching. These search into the past life of the preacher. But the sandals are bound round within with white leather ; so must the desire of the preacher be pure before God, out of a clean conscience ; and without appears the black, since the life of the preacher seems despised by them that are worldly on account of the myriad afflictions of this present life. The upper part of the sandal, through which the foot enters, is sewn together with many threads, that the two leather bands be not separated ; for at first the preacher should apply himself to the many virtues and

* So Mariott. The original word is *calcaneum*.

sayings of the Scriptures, that his outward acts may not be at variance with those which are secret and known to God only. The tongue of the sandals, which is over the foot, sets forth the tongue of the preacher. The line made by the craft of the shoemaker, stretching from the tongue of the sandal to its end, sets forth the perfection of the Gospel ; the lines proceeding from either side, the law and the prophets, which are repeated in the Gospels ; they are repeated at the middle line, which stretches to the end. The bands denote the mystery of Christ's Incarnation . . . .'

We have given this strange mixture of mysticism and observation at length for several reasons. First, it emphasizes a curious distinction between the shoes of different orders of clergy which is not often brought into notice. Secondly, it gives a very full, though somewhat obscure, description of the sandal in the author's time. And thirdly, it exemplifies the absurd lengths to which an author can go who endeavours to extract hidden meanings from simple and easily explicable facts. Here Amalarius endeavours to extract solemn truths even from the seams which the maker found necessary in joining two pieces of leather together. If some modern writers on archaeological subjects took timely warning from such a melancholy example, we should have fewer wild theories and more facts.

It is sad that most of Amalarius' successors

quietly put aside his elaborately argued piece of symbolism. Pseudo-Alcuin is content with the old idea of Rabanus, that the Gospel should be kept from what is earthy as the feet are kept from the ground, but not otherwise covered. Ivo practically quotes Rabanus word for word; and even Innocent III, who is usually original, has little further to offer beside the quotation: 'How beautiful are the feet of them that preach the gospel of peace!'

IX. *The Pall.*—The pall is a symbol of jurisdiction, which is worn by the Pope, and by him bestowed upon all archbishops.

The material of which the pall is made is white wool. Both the shape of the vestment and its ornamentation have undergone modifications since it was invented, even during the mediaeval period itself. Its earliest appearance, and all that is known of its origin, is described in the preceding chapter. The folding of the *pallium* must have given a little trouble whenever it was put on; and this must before long have suggested the shape which meets us in the mediaeval pall: that of a loop of cloth with two tails projecting from opposite points in its circumference. A slight difference is observable between palls represented early and those represented late in the mediaeval period. In the former the branches are almost horizontal, passing round the arms between the shoulder and

The Final Form of Vestments. 97

elbow; in the latter they pass over the shoulder. In the former case the pall resembles a **T**, in the

FIG. 12.—ST DUNSTAN. (From a manuscript in the Cottonian Library; showing early forms of pall and mitre.)

latter a **Y**, whether seen from before or behind the wearer.

In whichever form it appears, however, the pall was secured in its place by pins. At first, when the vestments were of simple description, these pins could be run through pall and chasuble without doing much damage; afterwards, however, when enrichments were heaped upon the chasuble, these pins were not run into that vestment at all, but through loops provided for the purpose. It was discovered, however, that the pall in its latest development would stay in its place quite as well without pins as with them, and the loops were therefore abandoned. As the pins were generally made of gold, with heads of precious stones, some reluctance was felt at abandoning them altogether, and accordingly they sank into the position which the maniple and other vestments assumed—that of being ornaments.

The length of the pendent tails shows considerable variety at different times. They are extremely long—often extravagantly so—in monuments dating between the eleventh and fourteenth centuries. After that date they were curtailed, and at present are not more than a foot long. There is a little button of lead sewn into the ends of the tails to make them hang properly.

The pall never displayed that tendency to elaborate adornment which distinguished the other vestments of the mediaeval age. Doubtless the fact that all palls were made at Rome, and but few were made at a time, prevented any great change in fashion. Some differences are, notwithstanding, noticeable. In the earliest representations of tailed palls there is to be seen a single cross at the

The Final Form of Vestments. 99

end of each tail ; the same cross is to be seen worked on early *oraria* and *mappulae*. But in mediaeval and modern times there is a difference. At present the pall has six crosses, one on each tail and four on the oval, worked in black. In the middle ages we find sometimes four, sometimes as many as eight, worked in purple.

The history of each individual pall is curious. On the morning of St Agnes's Day (January 21) in each year, two lambs are sent into Rome each in a basket, the baskets being slung over a horse's back. These lambs are chosen with special reference to whiteness and goodness. The horse is driven to the palace of the Pope, who comes to a window and makes the sign of the cross over the lambs, which are then conducted to the church of St Agnes without the walls. Here, gaily adorned with flowers and ribbons, they are brought up to the altar, and kept there till mass is sung. After mass (formerly at the *Agnus Dei*) the celebrant blesses the lambs, which are then handed over to the charge of the canons of St John Lateran, by whom they are sent back to the Pope. The Pope hands them on to the dean of his subdeacons, who delivers them up to a nunnery, where they are kept and fed. When they are shorn, the wool is woven by the nuns into palls. On the eve of the day of St Peter and St Paul these palls are taken to St Peter's, and there blessed after evensong, after which they are shut up in a silver-gilt box to wait till they are wanted for bestowal on a new archbishop.

Each archbishop on election must go to Rome in person to receive the pall, unless prevented by serious obstacles—when the latter is the case it is solemnly sent to him by the Pope. He is not permitted to engage in any episcopal duty before receiving the pall; afterwards the vestment is worn only at High Mass on the following days: Nativity, St Stephen, St John, Circumcision, Epiphany, Palm Sunday, Maundy Thursday, Holy Saturday, Easter Sunday, Monday and Tuesday, Ascension, Pentecost, Feasts of the Virgin, Nativity of St John the Baptist, all days of Apostles, All Saints, Dedications of Churches, principal local feasts in the diocese, Consecrations of Bishops, Ordinations of Clergy, Feast of the local Dedication, and the Anniversary of the wearer's consecration. The Pope, however, wears the pall at all times when he says mass.

The pall is the symbol of the archiepiscopal authority, therefore it may not be worn without express papal permission outside the limits of the jurisdiction of the archbishop.* When he dies, the pall is buried with him, but it is only placed

* We give a figure of an effigy in Mayence Cathedral to the memory of Albrecht von Brandenburg, who died in 1545. This effigy is remarkable, and probably unique, in represent-

The Final Form of Vestments. 101

on his shoulders if he be buried within his own province, otherwise it is folded and placed beneath his head.* The pall is the only vestment which may not be lent by one cleric to another.

---

ing the archbishop as wearing two palls. Although this is a convenient method of informing the world of the fact that the person commemorated held two archbishoprics (Mayence and Magdeburg), it is, of course, a solecism, as the pall of the one could not legally be worn within the precincts of the other, and *vice versâ*. This monument is especially valuable, as it clearly distinguishes between the cross-staff and the pastoral staff, which are often confused. See the account of the pastoral staff later on in the present chapter.

FIG· 13.

* It is well known that ecclesiastics were buried in their Eucharistic vestments, with a chalice and paten, the former often filled with wine. Much nonsense is talked nowadays of the piety of the mediaeval builders and undertakers, who put their best work where no human eye could see it. Unfortunately for this theory, the chalice and paten were usually cheap base metal (Canterbury affords one notable exception), and the vestments were often an inferior or worn-out set. Economy was considered then, as now.

We now come to a singular point in the history of the pall, and one which has so far baffled ecclesiologists to explain. Although the pall is generally regarded as the peculiar emblem of archbishops, and seems to have been kept for their especial and peculiar use by the rites which we have described, yet a few favoured bishops have from very early times been entitled to wear this vestment. The bishoprics which possess this privilege are those of Autun, Bamberg, Dol, Lucca, Ostia, Pavia, and Verona.

The pall is represented on several monuments of bishops of these dioceses, *e.g.*, the slab of Bishop Otto (1192) and the brass of Bishop Lambert (1399), both in Bamberg Cathedral. In illuminated manuscripts and elsewhere we often find figures of clerics of episcopal rank wearing the pall, but holding the crook-headed staff, commonly supposed to be the insignia of a *bishop* as distinguished from an archbishop; but as numerous examples exist to show that the latter notion (like the majority of popular ideas in archaeology) is erroneous, this combination proves nothing.

The peculiar circumstances distinguishing the pall from the rest of the ecclesiastical vestments would lead us to expect some remarkable disquisitions on its symbolism. This expectation is not disappointed. The cross on the back and front reminds the wearer to reflect piously and in a worthy manner on the Passion of the Redeemer, and holds up before the people the sign of their Redemption. Such is the old view, and it has at least the merit of simplicity and religious feeling. But, unfortunately, Amalarius, in his dissecting manner, draws a parallel between the pall and the golden plate of the Levitical High Priest; this clears the way for the extraordinary disquisition of the pseudo-Alcuin on the Tetragrammaton יהוה' (as he inaccurately writes it), wherein *Jod* signifies 'principium,' *He* 'iste,' *Vau* 'vita,' and *Heth* 'passio'—'id est, iste est principium passionis vitae.' Honorius thinks, however, that the four letters typify the four arms of the cross. Innocent III and others tell us that the pall signifies that discipline with which archbishops should rule themselves and those set under them. As Innocent's account of the pall gives as full an account as can be obtained of the vestment and its ornamentation and fastenings, we give an abstract of it here:

'The pall which the principal bishops wear signifies the discipline with which archbishops should rule themselves aud those set under them. By this the golden chain* is obtained which those receive who strive lawfully, of which Solomon saith, " My son, hear the instruction of thy father and forsake not the law of thy mother, for they

* A not uncommon comparison for the loop of the pall.

shall be an ornament of grace unto thy head and chains about thy neck." For the pallium is made of white wool, woven, having a circle above constraining the shoulders, and two tails (*lineae*) hanging down on either side; moreover, there are four purple crosses, front and back, on the right and on the left. On the left side it is double, and single on the right.'* After a long moralization on these facts, he goes on : 'The three pins which are fixed in the pallium over the breast, on the shoulder and in the back, denote pity for his neighbour, the administration of his office, and the meting out of justice. . . . There is no pin fastened in the right shoulder,' because there is no trouble in everlasting rest. 'The needle is golden, sharp below, rounded above, enclosing a precious stone,' which bears a variety of meanings. If we may believe the Elizabethan reformers, the pall was an expensive item in an archbishop's insignia. Although Gregory I ordained that it should be given to the archbishop-elect freely, Jewel speaks of the Archbishop of Canterbury giving 5,000 florins (£1,125 at 4s. 6d. the florin) to the Pope for his pall, in addition to the first-fruits of his province; and Bullinger speaks of the pall being so dear that 'in gathering money for it' the archbishop often 'beggared his whole diocese.'

X. *The Stockings*, or buskins, seem to have

* A survival of the old method of wearing it.

been originally appropriated to the Pope alone, bishops being content with the somewhat scanty sandal already described. But by the time of Ivo of Chartres the *caligae* had taken their place among the articles in an episcopal wardrobe. He is the first writer who mentions them. In the middle ages they, like all the other vestments of which we have been treating, forsook their primitive simplicity and became enriched with elaborate ornamentation. They signify the need of framing the courses of their feet aright; and in that they reach to the knees, they indicate that the wearer should strengthen the feeble knees weakened by heedlessness, and hasten to preach the Gospel.

FIG. 14.—BISHOP WAYNFLETE'S EPISCOPAL STOCKING.

XI. *The Subcingulum.*—The discussion of this vestment will be more difficult than that of any other among the equipment of the clergy of the West. It is all but obsolete at the present day; there does not seem to be more than one representation of it extant, and that only shows a small portion of it in an unsatisfactory manner; and the references to it in ecclesiastical writers are few and far between.

In antiquarian or any other investigations it is invariably the best rule, when a puzzle is set for solution, to work backwards from the known to the unknown. We will follow this course in speaking of this vestment, and commence with a description of it as worn at the present day.

The modern *subcingulum* is reserved for the exclusive use of the Pope. It takes the form of a girdle, passed round the alb, and having on the left side a maniple-like appendage. This seems to have been the form which it had in the end of the fourteenth century, for in an 'Ordo Missae Pontificalis,' published by Georgi,* we read: 'Primo induit (pontifex) sibi albam, deinde cinctorium cum manipulo ad sinistram partem.' In the century before this Durandus, in his 'Rationale Divinorum Officiorum,' writes: 'Sane a sinistro latere pontificis ex cingulo duplex dependet succinctorium '†—a doubled 'apron' hangs on the left hand side; and he likens it to a quiver, in the course of an elaborate comparison between the episcopal vestments of his time and the spiritual armour of the Christian.

The *succinctorium* must have adopted this form

* Liturgia Rom. Pont., vol. iii, p. 556; *cit. ap.* Rock, Church of Our Fathers.

† Rationale, III 4.

The Final Form of Vestments. 107

about the middle of the thirteenth century. At the beginning of that century we find that it had its use, and was not a mere ornament. In the 'Ordo Romanus' of Cencio de Sabellis, written at the end of the twelfth century,* is a description of the new Pope's taking possession of the Church of St John Lateran. He is there described as being 'girt with a belt of crimson silk, hanging from which is a purple *purse* (bursa) containing twelve precious stones and some musk.' These all had their symbolical meaning: the belt denoted purity, the purse almsgiving, the stones the apostles, the musk 'a good odour in the sight of God.'

Innocent III, writing at the commencement of the thirteenth century, describes the vestment as peculiar to *bishops*, but does not refer to it as peculiar to *popes*; neither, be it noticed, does Cencio. The last restriction may have crept in one or two centuries after Innocent. He does not enter into many details concerning it, but he clearly distinguishes it from the *zona*, or girdle, which denotes continence, as the *subcingulum* signifies abstinence.†

About this time a fresco was executed on the

---

* Printed in Mabillon, Musei Ital., ii, p. 212.

† Were it not for this, we might infer from the other passages quoted that the succintorium was simply hung on the ordinary girdle.

wall of the *Sagro Speco* at Subiaco, which remains till the present day. It represents a Pope fully vested, but under the folds of the chasuble on either side is a fretted ornament which is certainly not part of any of the ordinary vestments of any rank of clergy. There is no alternative but to regard Dr Rock as correct in considering this ornament as part of the sub-cingulum.

FIG. 15.—FIGURE OF A POPE. (*Temp.* INNOCENT III.)

This being granted, the sub-cingulum is seen to be a girdle, from either side of which depends a lozenge-shaped 'lappet.' We shall meet with a similar lappet in the ἐπιγονάτιον of the Greek Church. Only portions of these lappets are to be seen in the fresco in question, but enough is apparent to show them to be lozenge-shaped.

The testimony of Cencio points to these lappets being, not mere ornaments, but bags or purses hung to the belt; and this brings us to another stage in the evolution of this vestment. We know that through the middle ages a bag called a *gypcière* hung at the belts of civilians, and served the double purpose of purse and pocket. It is but natural to suppose that the early clergy found such appendages useful even in divine service. Let us now go yet further, and see whether confirmation of these theories awaits us.

Honorius of Autun in 1130 writes: 'The subcingulum, also called perizona or subcinctorium, is hung doubled about the loins; this signifies zeal in almsgiving,' etc.

Note, in this passage, the expression 'hung doubled.' This can only refer to the 'lappets' being hung *one on each side*. And the 'almsgiving,' which Honorius asserts this vestment to signify, suggests a purse.

Other writers, in the century preceding Honorius, write to the same effect; and even as early as the tenth century, in a manuscript of the mass, we find a distinction drawn between the 'cingulum' and the 'baltheum' in the prayers said while vesting.

In short, it seems probable that the subcingulum, with its appendages, is, like several other sacerdotal vestments, a modification into an ornament of something which had been designed for some natural requirement. When the maniple became too narrow and too richly embroidered to be of the slightest use as a handkerchief, it cannot be supposed that the priest did entirely without some resource; some plain piece of cloth must surely have been employed in its place, and some pocket must then have been required in which to place it. Again, some receptacle must have been wanted in which to place those comforting metal 'apples' in which hot water was placed when the day was cold; and the thumbstall or ponser, the thimble designed to keep the oil which adhered to his thumb after it had been dipped in the chrism, from greasing any of his vestments. It seems only natural to suppose that the subcingulum was originally designed to supply these wants.

XII. *The Rational.*— This ornament, obsolete now, was assumed by the bishops of the early years of the middle ages, in direct imitation of the breastplate of the ephod worn by the Jewish High Priest.

It consisted of a wooden brooch, overlaid with enamelled metal, which was fastened high up on the breast of the chasuble, and seems commonly to have been worn when there was no central orphrey on that vestment.

The shape and ornamentation of the rational varied altogether with the caprice of the artist who designed it. Examples are extremely rare in inventories of cathedral goods, if, indeed, they occur at all. It is probable that they were catalogued together with the *morses* of copes, with which they were practically identical in appearance.

The word 'Rationale' first meets us in the

The Final Form of Vestments. 111

expression 'rationale judicii,' used in the Vulgate *passim* as a translation of the τὸ λογεῖον τῆς κρίσεως, by which the Septuagint expressed the breastplate of the ephod. In the early Church writers the word 'judicii' was dropped and 'rationale' used alone, but always to denote the Jewish ornament. When pseudo-Alcuin wrote, in the tenth or eleventh century, the ecclesiastical rational was quite unknown, for he says : ' Pro rationali summi pontifices, quos archiepiscopos dicemus, pallio utuntur '—a statement which he would certainly not have made if anything less unlike the rational than the pallium had been known to him. Ivo of Chartres, too, knows nothing of the Christian ornament, for although he does not say definitely that the Jewish rational corresponded to the pallium, he says that it corresponded to an ornament *conceded* (*concessum*) to the chief bishops of his time—an expression which would define the pallium, but certainly not the rational. Honorius of Autun is the writer in whom we first meet with direct and unequivocal mention of the ornament; and he begins his remarks upon it by definitely stating : 'Rationale a Lege est sumptum'—*Lege*, of course, being the Levitical law. This gives us very closely the limits of date between which the rational was assumed—some time between 1100 and 1130.

The rational, if we may accept the testimony

of the monuments, gradually died out about the fourteenth or fifteenth century. It seems never to have been universal, and an actual rational is one of the rarest ecclesiological treasures a collector can possess.

XIII. *The Mitre.*—Like that of the *subcingulum*, the history of the mitre is a curious piece of evolution; but, unlike the *subcingulum*, the mitre can be traced through all its history in an unbroken chain of literary references, monumental effigies, and actual specimens.

The word *mitra* (Gk. μίτος, *a thread*) is applied in the transitional period to a female head-dress, and even St Isidore of Seville makes use of the word in that sense. The Septuagint, however, occasionally translates the expression for the cap of the high priest by μίτρα; at other times they use the word κίδαρις, which they also apply to the cap of the second order of the Jewish priesthood. The Vulgate follows the Septuagint, sometimes using *mitra*, sometimes *cidaris*, and occasionally *tiara*.

The advocates of an origin in primitive antiquity for Ecclesiastical Vestments make much of two passages which are certainly obscure, and would seem to indicate that in apostolic times 'bishops' wore a *gold plate* upon their heads. These passages are in a letter sent by Polycrates of Ephesus to Victor, bishop of Rome, about the year 200 A.D., in which he alludes to St John as 'having become a priest wearing the gold plate' ἐγενήθη ἱερεὺς τὸ πέταλον πεφορηκώς;* and in the writings of Epiphanius of Salamis (*circa* 400 A.D.), in which he says of James, the brother of Our Lord, that he was a priest after the ancient rite, and was permitted to wear a gold plate—ἱερατεύσαντα αὐτὸν κατὰ τὴν παλαιὰν ἱερωσύνη εὕρομεν . . . καὶ τὸ πέταλον ἐπὶ τῆς κεφαλῆς ἐξῆν αὐτῷ φερεῖν,† citing the authority of Eusebius, Clement, and others. These statements are so hopelessly vague and confused that very little can be made out of them, but it has been pointed out that (i) the passages in which they occur are largely allegorical, (ii) that the πέταλον seems to refer to the gold plate of Jewish priesthood, and that the expression 'priest with the πέταλον' probably was used currently in the early years of Christianity, much as 'mitred abbot' is by us at the present day. In any case, as Dr Sinker says,‡ it 'is plain enough that if St John and St James, or either of them, did wear this ornament, it was an ornament 'special to themselves and ceased with them, affecting in no sense the further use of the church.'

* Ap. Eusebius, Hist. Eccl., v 24; Migne, Patrol. Graec., xx 493.

† Contra Haer., I xxix 4; Migne, Patrol. Graec., xli 396.

‡ In Smith and Cheetham's 'Dictionary of Christian Antiquities,' s.v. *mitre.*

Other passages, supposed to refer to this or similar practices, bearing dates between the fourth and sixth centuries, are found on examination to have no real bearing on the question. The number of extracts from writers of that time which have been brought forward to prove the antiquity of the mitre is considerable; but those which can at all bear consideration apart from their contexts are all vague, unconvincing and inconclusive; some, indeed, are so obviously figurative that their production is only an amusing illustration of the straits to which the believers in the elaboration of primitive ritual are reduced. And the evidence of Tertullian on the other side is very clear—'quis denique patriarches, quis prophetes, quis levites, aut sacerdos, aut archon, quis vel postea apostolus aut evangelizator aut episcopus invenitur coronatus?'[*]

In the face of this quotation it is not easy to see what to make of the passages in St Jerome and elsewhere, in which a bishop is addressed by the expression 'corona vestra,' much as we use the words 'your lordship' now. Dr Rock argues from this that bishops, even so early as the fifth century, wore a circlet or crown of gold at Divine service. If so, the use must have been confined to Rome, for otherwise the Toletan or other

[*] 'De Corona Militis,' cap. ix. Migne, ii 88.

councillors would surely have given us definite information concerning it.

St Isidore of Seville, in his treatise 'De Officiis Ecclesiasticis,' book ii, chap. vii, describes the tonsure as indicative of the priesthood and the regal nature of the church, the shaven part of the head representing the hemispherical cap of the Jewish priests, and the circlet of hair representing the coronet of kings. It is true that he is not speaking definitely of bishops, but the fact that he is absolutely silent respecting a crown of any kind other than the crown of hair—for which he expressly uses the word *corona*—is at least presumptive evidence that the crown of gold was not worn in his day. The prophecy of King Laoghairé's druids affords a very curious corroboration of this; see *post*, p. 128.

The earliest representation that Dr Rock can adduce of an ecclesiastic wearing this circlet is a figure in the Benedictional of St Aethelwold, an MS. of the tenth century at Chatsworth. Here we have a figure, the brows of which are certainly encircled with a gold band set with precious stones. As Marriott points out, however, this is probably more of a secular than an ecclesiastical nature, and may indicate the royal rank to which bishops at that time frequently laid claim.

Menard, after a careful study of ancient liturgies, came to the conclusion that the mitre was not in use in the church prior to the year 1000. Contemporary art bears out this statement. Probably the earliest genuine representation of a bishop wearing a head-dress to which any importance can be attached from a liturgical point of view is an illumination of St Dunstan* in an MS. (Claud. A 3) in the British Museum. This is of the early years of the eleventh century. It shows us a simple cap, low and hemispherical in shape, without the least trace of the cleft now invariably associated with the episcopal headgear.

The fashion seems to have changed with considerable rapidity, and the cleft very soon began to make its appearance. Its first beginning was a very shallow, blunt depression between two low, blunt, rounded points, one over each ear—in fact, a depression such as would naturally be made in a soft cloth cap by passing the outstretched hand gently across the crown. This change was not long in giving place to another and more important modification. The mitre was turned so that the horns appeared one in front, one behind, and they were raised a little higher than before, and, instead of being rounded, were made of a triangular form. The mitre in this shape is that universally represented in MSS. of the twelfth century.

Little difference in shape is traceable in the

* See fig. 12, p. 97.

The Final Form of Vestments. 117

mitres of the thirteenth, fourteenth, fifteenth or sixteenth centuries. During these four hundred years the mitre increased considerably in size, but

FIG. 16.—A BISHOP, SALISBURY CATHEDRAL (Jocelyn, Twelfth Century).

FIG. 17.—AN ARCHBISHOP, MAYENCE CATHEDRAL (Diether von Isenburg, 1482).

it was reserved for the seventeenth century to stereotype the final modification in form. Hitherto the two horns of the mitre had as a general rule been in the shape of plain triangles, bent round so as to adapt themselves to the outline of the head ; the mitre was thus cylindrical in outline. By the seventeenth century, however, the triangles had been made spherical, so that the mitre assumed the form of a pair of parentheses, or of a barrel, which it still possesses.* By this time it had grown to a considerable height—some eighteen inches.

When the mitre was a plain cloth cap it was kept in position by two ribbons, which were knotted at the back of the head. The end of these ribbons are well shown in the figure of St Dunstan. But the ribbons very early lost their usefulness and became simple ornaments, and the ubiquitous embroiderer was not long in seizing on these *infulae*, or lappets, and enriching them with needlework to the best of her ability.

The mitre was originally made of plain white linen, and until about the twelfth century continued to be so ; it was occasionally, though by no means always, elaborately decorated with needlework. Such simplicity, however, was not consistent with the spirit of the age which followed, and we find that in the thirteenth century the mitre was made of silk, and invariably overlaid either with embroidery

* Traces of a slight 'bulge' are discernible in a few examples of even so early a date as the fifteenth century. It is well developed in von Brandenburg's effigy, figured on p. 101.

The Final Form of Vestments. 119

or pearls and other jewels. To such a length was this enrichment carried at last in England, that we read that Henry VIII removed from Fountains Abbey, among other treasures, a silver-gilt mitre set with pearl and stone—weight seventy ounces!

Although properly belonging to the seventh chapter, in which the ritual uses of the various vestments which we have been describing will be discussed, it is necessary here to detail the three classes into which mitres are divided. Unlike other vestments, which are classified according to the particular liturgical *colour* which predominates in their embroidery, mitres are classified according to the *manner* in which they are ornamented. The background, when it can be seen at all, is white. A mitre which is simply made of white linen or silk, with little or no enrichment, is called a *mitra simplex*; one ornamented richly with embroidery, but without precious metals or stones, is called a *mitra aurifrigiata*; and one in which precious metals and stones are employed in its decoration is called a *mitra pretiosa.* The different times at which these different kinds of mitres are worn will be noted in their proper place in Chapter VII.

The papal tiara may be briefly described in this place. It first appears about the eleventh century as a conical cap, encircled with a single crown at

Fig. 18.—Pastoral Staff and Mitra Pretiosa (the Limerick Mitre).

the brow; assumed about the time of the growth of the earthly power of the papacy, it may well be regarded as symbolical of spiritual and temporal rule. The subsequent modifications through which it passed were few in number, though considerable in character: they consisted in the addition of a second crown by Boniface VIII (1300 A.D.), of a third by Urban V (1362-70), and the swelling out of the body of the head-dress into a bulging form about the sixteenth century, much about the time when the mitre assumed the same shape.

XIV. *The Episcopal Gloves.* — These undoubtedly owe their invention to the coldness and cheerlessness of the early churches, and were invented simply to keep the hands of the wearer warm. But about the ninth century they, with so many similar vestments, assumed a more sacred character, and a prayer was prescribed for putting them on, as was the case with the other and better established vestments. They do not appear to be formally mentioned as vestments till the time of Honorius of Autun, who draws moral lessons from them.

Throughout the middle ages the gloves were richly embroidered and jewelled; often a large stone is to be seen on the back of each hand.

The gloves (*chirothecae*, or *manicae*) must be carefully distinguished from the *manicae* or *brachialia*, the sleeves of coarse cloth which the bishop used to draw over his arm to protect the apparels of his alb from the water when administering baptism by immersion.

As the hands are sometimes covered with gloves and sometimes bare, so good deeds should be sometimes hidden to prevent self-sufficiency, and sometimes revealed as an edifying example to those near us. So says Honorius of Autun ; perhaps this is as satisfactory an exegesis as has ever been given of the gloves or any other vestment.

XV. *The Episcopal Ring.*—Although, as we have seen, the ring was recognised as one of the special marks of a bishop at the time of the fourth council of Toledo, and was regarded by St Isidore of Seville as a special article used in the investiture of a bishop, none of the liturgical writers of the earliest years of the mediaeval period notices it ; not till we come to Honorius of Autun is any mention of it to be found. The reason of this is not far to seek, and has been given by Marriott. Rabanus, Amalarius, Ivo, and the rest, occupied themselves more or less with the supposed connexion between the liturgical and the Jewish vestments, and therefore, as they were not writing treatises dealing solely with Christian vestments, they omitted all mention of ornaments which had no direct bearing on the questions with which they were engaged. Hence, both the ring and pastoral staff suffered, as the most ingenious torturing could not extract anything in the Levitical rites analogous to these important insignia.

The evidence of the monuments is conclusive on two points. First, that the episcopal ring proper was only one of a large number of rings worn by the bishop, the others being probably purely ornamental and secular; second, that it was worn on the third finger of the right hand, and *above* the second joint of that finger, not being passed, as rings are now, down to the knuckle. It was usually kept in place with a plain guard ring.

The ring was always a circlet with a precious stone, never engraved, and it was large enough to pass over the gloved finger. The stone was usually a sapphire, sometimes an emerald or a ruby.

Although the ring is distinguishable, by its position on the right hand as well as by other circumstances, from the wedding-ring, Honorius of Autun (after referring to the ring placed on the finger of the Prodigal Son and the wedding ring of iron with an adamantine stone forged by 'a certain wise man called Prometheus') has been trapped into saying that the bishop wears a ring that he may declare himself the bridegroom of the church and may lay down his life for it, should necessity arise, as did Christ.

XVI. *The Pastoral Staff.* — We have briefly sketched the probable origin of the pastoral staff in the preceding chapter, and come now to discuss the forms it presented and the connexions in which it was used during the middle ages. As there is no department of the study of Ecclesiastical Vestments about which so much popular misconception exists, it will be necessary to enter into these details at considerable length.

As utterly unfounded as the common notions concerning 'low-side windows' and crossed-legged effigies is the idea that the differences in the positions of pastoral staves as represented in sculptured monuments have any meaning whatsoever, secret or personal. A pastoral staff remains a pastoral staff, and nothing more, whether it is on the right side of the bearer or on the left, and whether its crook is turned inwards or outwards.

Synonymous with 'pastoral staff' is the word *crozier* or *crosier;* but it is frequently ignorantly applied to a totally different object—the cross-staff borne before an archbishop. The statements which we so often see in works professing to treat on ecclesiological subjects as to the pastoral staff being crook-headed and borne by bishops, the crozier cross-headed, and borne (instead of the pastoral staff) *by* archbishops, are derived from a misunderstanding of the evidence of mediaeval monuments.* The truth is, that the pastoral staff, with which the crozier is identical, is borne by bishops and archbishops alike ; but archbishops are distinguished from bishops by having a staff, with a cross or crucifix in its head, borne *before* them in addition. In many monuments, it is true, archbishops are represented as carrying the cross-staff, as, for instance, the brass of Archbishop Cranley in New College, Oxford ; but it was obviously impossible in a monument of this kind to represent a cross-bearer preceding the archbishop, and the slight inaccuracy was, therefore, perpetrated of making the archbishop bear his own cross, thereby substantiating the evidence of the *pall*, that the person represented was of higher rank than that of a bishop. It was better managed at Mayence, where, in the monument of Albrecht von Brandenburg, 1545, figured above (p. 101), the figure is represented as bearing both the crozier and the cross-staff, one in each hand ; and at Bamberg, in the cathedral of which city is a brass to Bishop Lambert von Brunn† (1399), wherein he is represented holding the crozier in his left hand, the cross-staff in his right.

* This blunder has even crept into the ninth edition of the 'Encyclopaedia Britannica.'

† The bishops of Bamberg had a right to wear the archi-episcopal pontificalia. See p. 102, *ante*.

In the earliest representations of a staff of office there is a considerable variety in the shape of the head; knobs, crooks, and even Y-shapes, all meet us. The shape probably depended on the shape of the branch of the tree from which the staff was cut, much as does the shape of an ordinary walking-stick. By St Isidore's time, however, the crook-head had become stereotyped; the number of exceptional forms which we find after that date is small. There is a considerable number of staves of about the eleventh century, either represented on monuments or actually existing, of which the heads are tau-shaped; these possibly betray Eastern influence. A few effigies or pictures of bishops remain with a knob-headed staff; an example is to be seen in a ninth-century Anglo-Saxon pontifical at Rouen.

The crook-headed staff is, however, by far the commonest, and after the eleventh century the only, form in which the bishop's crozier is found. Some variety is discoverable in the extent to which the staff is crooked. In some —notably in Irish specimens — the head is shaped like an inverted U, the form of the whole staff being that represented in the annexed diagram; but in the great majority of instances the head is recurved into a spiral or volute.

In the Irish form of crozier the front is flat, and shaped like an oval shield. This is often move able, disclosing a hollow behind it, which was almost certainly used as a reliquary.*

The materials of which the pastoral staff was made were very diverse. The stick was of wood, usually some precious wood, such as cedar, cypress, or ebony. This wood was often gilt or overlaid with silver plates. In the twelfth century the staff was shod with iron and surmounted with a knob of crystal, above which the crook proper was attached. The crook-head of the Irish crozier was of bronze; that of the other form generally of carved ivory. When the process of elaboration was felt in this as in all the other sacerdotal ornaments, the stick as well as the head was often carved from ivory, and either gilt or silvered heavily, and set with precious stones. Beneath the crook were often niches or shrines, containing figures of saints.

The bronze Irish crozier was decorated with the marvellous interlacing knots and bands which are the special glory of early Irish Christian art. On the flat front is often to be seen a plain cross, at the centre of which is a setting for a precious stone, and in each quarter an interlacing band. In the volute form of crozier a different style of ornamentation was adopted; the surface was not

* The ordinary form of crozier was not unknown in Ireland; the well-known crozier of Cashel is a beautiful specimen. The crook form was, however, earlier.

ornamented, but the head was carved into solid forms; in the centre of the volute was usually represented some sacred person or scene, real or legendary, or else some symbolical device or conventional patterns. It is hard to say which of these two forms of crozier is the better from an aesthetic point of view. The graceful curve of the volute certainly compares favourably with the somewhat stiff outline of the Irish crozier; but the feebleness of even the best mediaeval attempts at representing the human figure in miniature considerably detracts from the artistic value of the volute crozier when a human figure is introduced; while, on the other hand, the incomparable excellence of the Irish metal-workers transformed the U-shaped crozier into an object of great beauty. The lines of the knots are always faultlessly executed, and the ornamentation is invariably in good taste.*

* This form of crozier is no doubt contemplated in the prophecy attributed to the druids of Laoghairé, King of Ireland, as cited in the law-tract known as the *Senchus Mór*—

'Tiucfaid Tailginn tar muir meirginn
A croinn cromcinn, a cinn tollcinn
A miasa in airthiur atighe,' etc.—

that is, 'the Tonsured ones shall come through the stormy sea, their staves crook-headed, their heads tonsured, their tables in the east of their houses,' etc. It is worth noting, apropos of what was said on p. 115 respecting the bishop's *corona*, that the words 'a cinn tollcinn'—'their heads tonsured,' are thus glossed in the MS.—'.i. a coirne ina cennaib'—'*i.e.*, their *crowns* on their heads.'

The Final Form of Vestments.

The following copy of the Lincoln Inventory of pastoral staves (1536) illustrates some of the points already noticed. It also indicates that the head and staff of the crozier were separable, and, when stored in the vestry, kept apart from one another :

'In primis a hede of one busshopes staffe of sylver and gylte w^t one knop and perles & other stones havyng a Image of ow^r savyow^r of the one syde and a Image of sent John Baptiste of the other syde wanting xxj stones & perles w^t one bose [boss] and one sokett weyng xviij unces.

'Item one other hede of a staffe copo^r & gylte.

'Item a staffe ordend for one of the seyd hedes the wyche ys ornate w^t stones sylver and gylte and iij circles, a boute the staffe sylver and gylte wantyng vij stones.

'Item a staffe of horn and wod for the hede of copo^r.

'Item j staff covered w^t silver wthout heeid.'

In the corresponding inventory of Winchester Cathedral we find entered three pastoral staves silver-gilt, one pastoral staff of a 'unicorn's' (presumably a narwhal's) horn and four pastoral staves of plates of silver.

Suspended to the top of the staff was a streamer or napkin, which, like the lappet of the mitre, was called the *infula*. This was originally introduced to keep the moisture of the hand from tarnishing the metal of the staff. The symbolists think it is a 'banner' of some sort or other.

It will be convenient, before proceeding to the discussion of the next vestment on our list, to give a few particulars regarding the archbishop's cross. This is necessary owing to the confusion already noticed, which exists between the crozier and the cross ; but as the cross cannot strictly be included in a catalogue of ecclesiastical vestments, we shall make our notes as brief as possible.

The custom of preceding an archbishop with a cross was introduced throughout the Western Church about the beginning of the twelfth century. It was carried by one of the archbishop's chaplains, who in this country received the name of 'croyser,' or cross-bearer, for that reason. The cross was usually richly ornamented with metal-work and jewels, and often, if not always, bore a figure of Our Lord on each face, so that the eyes of the archbishop were fixed on the one, those of the people on the other.

The circumstance of highest importance connected with the archbishop's cross, so far as it concerns our present purpose, is this : the prelate *never* bore the cross himself, except on the one occasion of his investiture. He then received the cross into his own hands, but immediately passed it on to his cross-bearer.

The Pope is often in mediaeval monuments and illustrations represented as preceded by a cross with three transoms of different length, the uppermost being the shortest, the lowermost the longest. This is simply the result of a desire on the part of the artist to improve upon the patriarch's cross of the Eastern Church, which *appears* to have two transoms, the upper transom being in point of fact a representation of the board on which the superscription on the cross was written.

One more staff may be worth a passing mention—the staff borne as an emblem of authority by the ruler of the choir, who looked after the singing and behaviour of the boys. This was of silver, with a cross-head.

The false conceptions about the crozier have probably arisen from an inaccurate etymological analogy with the word *cross*. The true derivation connects it with such words as our *crotchet* and *crook*.

The symbolism of the shepherd's staff is naturally the leading thought in the minds of the mystics. It was probably, however, considered too obvious, and they cast about to find yet further secret meanings. Thus, Honorius notices that the Lord commanded the apostles to 'take nothing save a staff only' when they were going out to preach, and then says that 'the staff which sustains the feeble signifies the authority of teaching,' and much more to the same effect. Innocent III says that the point is sharp, the middle straight, the top curved, to indicate that the priest should spur on the idle, rule the weak, collect the wandering. He further explains the fact that the Pope does not bear the pastoral staff by telling us that 'the blessed St Peter sent his staff to Eucharius, the first bishop of Trèves, whom he had sent, together with Valerius and Maternus, to preach the Gospel among the Germans. Maternus succeeded him in the bishopric; he had been raised from the dead by the staff of St Peter. And this staff is preserved with great reverence in the church of Trèves.' St Thomas Aquinas supplements this piece of information by telling us that for this reason the Pope carries the pastoral staff when pontificating in Trèves.*

The episcopal staff is alleged to have borne the following inscriptions: round the crook, 'Cum iratus fueris misericordiae recordaberis'; on the ball below the crook, 'Homo'; on the spike at the bottom, 'Parce.' By these inscriptions the bishop was warned that he was but a man himself; that in wrath he should remember mercy; and that he should spare, even when administering discipline. Whether these warnings were invariably effective is a matter into which we will not inquire.

XVII. *The Tunicle.*—This was simply a small variety of the dalmatic, appropriated to the use of subdeacons and bishops.

It differed from the dalmatic merely in being somewhat smaller. It was made of silk or of

* Sentent. IV, dist. 24, quaest. 3, art. 3, *ad fin.* ed. Parmae (1873), vol. vii, p. 913.

wool, and first appears about the year 820 as a subdeacon's vestment; but it is considerably later than this that it appears as a bishop's garment. In the ninth century bishops appear with but one vestment — the alba — under the chasuble; between the ninth and eleventh centuries the dalmatic makes its appearance; and it is not till about 1200 that we find the tunicle illustrated in paintings or effigies of bishops. A reference to the table given in the early part of the present chapter will show that the literary evidence points in the same direction.

The tunicle did not escape the common fate of all the vestments of the mediaeval church, and it, too, became overlaid with needlework, first in a strip across the breast of the subdeacon, then (as this would not show under the vestments of the bishop) on the rest of the surface. The tunicle on Bishop Goodrick's brass at Ely Cathedral—one of the latest representations of this vestment in England—is as richly embroidered as the dalmatic.

In a few episcopal effigies of the thirteenth century the dalmatic alone appears. The tunicle being worn beneath the dalmatic, and being naturally smaller, was hidden. This difficulty was, however, very soon surmounted by the simple process of shortening the dalmatic.

Properly, the dalmatic only is fringed; the tunicle of the subdeacon seldom, if ever, shows this manner of ornamentation. But in the later episcopal effigies it is by no means uncommon.

XVIII. *The Orale,* or, as it is now called, the *Fanon,* is described by Dr Rock as 'an oblong piece of white silk gauze of some length, striped across its width with narrow bars, alternately gold, blue, and red. . . . It is cast upon the head of the Pope like a hood, and its two ends are wrapped one over the right, the other over the left shoulder, and thus kept until the holy father is clad in the chasuble, when the fanon is thrown back and made to hang smoothly and gracefully above and all around the shoulders of that vestment, like a tippet.'

From the orale being supposed to represent the ephod, as well as from the manner of its being put on, it is probable that it was an evolution from the amice. It is not mentioned by liturgical writers before Innocent III, and does not appear in paintings or monuments of much older date; it therefore seems to have been assumed about the twelfth or thirteenth century.

XIX. *The Pectoral Cross.*—We must not omit to mention this important episcopal ornament. As an official ornament it is of comparatively late introduction; it first appears in the pages of Innocent III and Durandus, and from the references which these liturgiologists make to it, it was evidently regarded by them as exclusively

The Final Form of Vestments. 135

confined to the Pope's use. Thus, Innocent says: 'Romanus autem pontifex post albam et cingulum assumit orale, quod circa caput involvit et replicat super humeros' for certain symbolic reasons; 'et quia signo crucis auri lamina cessit pro lamina quam pontifex ille [Judaeus] gerebat in fronte, pontifex iste crucem gerit in pectore.' Dr Rock has been unable to find any trace of the pectoral cross appearing on the breast of an ordinary bishop before the sixteenth century. Even by the Popes it appears before this time to have been covered by the chasuble. Probably the cross was originally a reliquary.

On p. 29 we referred to a MS. of uncertain date in the monastery of St Martin at Autun, which details the vestments worn in the Gallican church in (probably) the tenth century. This gives a somewhat different catalogue from the lists of the rest of the Western Church, and displays some Eastern influence. The *pallium, casula, alba*, and *stola* are described so that they appear identical with the corresponding vestments elsewhere; the maniple also appears, under the name *vestimentum parvolum;* and we have in addition the *manualia* or *manicae*, which do not appear in any other Western lists; they are said in the MS. to have been regularly worn 'like bracelets,' and to have covered the arms of 'kings and priests.' This points to vestments after the style of the ἐπιμανίκια of the Greeks, which will be noticed in their proper place in Chapter V.

We have now described the vestments worn by the priests of the Western Church at the Eucharistic service, and are thus in a position to give a satisfactory answer to the question, 'Were they adaptations of the Jewish, or natural evolutions of the Roman costume?' We have seen that the jeweller, the goldsmith, and the embroiderer conspired to make the vestments of the middle ages as gorgeous as possible, and that therein, and in some few other particulars, they resembled the Mosaic costume; but as we go back nearer and nearer to the first ages of Christianity all the glitter drops off, vestment after vestment disappears, till we reach the three plain white vestments of the fourth century, from which it is but a step to the ordinary costume of a Roman citizen of good position during the second or third century of our era. We have also seen that all attempts at drawing hidden meanings from the vestments fail; the results, when not far-fetched, are contradictory and unconvincing.

CHAPTER IV.

THE HISTORY AND CHARACTERISTICS OF THE
PROCESSIONAL VESTMENTS; THE ORNAMENTA-
TION OF VESTMENTS.

IN addition to the garments already described, which are more properly appropriated to the Eucharistic service, there are a few which are assumed on other occasions by the clergy of the Western Church. The occasions upon which these particular vestments are worn belong properly to the province of Chapter VII. We accordingly postpone the discussion of them until that chapter is reached, concerning ourselves here with the development, shape, and ornamentation of the vestments themselves.

The vestments which we have to describe in this chapter are the cassock, surplice (with its modifications, the rochet and cotta), almuce, and cope. These constitute the so-called processional vestments; a misnomer, because they are not exclusively appropriated to processions. There are, besides, certain others of a more general character, not strictly falling under the head of either Eucharistic or Processional vesture, and they will be more conveniently described in this chapter also. These are the canon's cope, the mozetta, the Roman collar, and the various types of sacerdotal headdress.

I. *The Cassock.* — The cassock was the long outer gown which was worn by everyone, clerical and lay, male and female, during the eleventh, twelfth, and succeeding centuries. When it was abandoned for the very much more convenient short coat, that conservatism in ecclesiastical matters, to which the very existence of ecclesiastical vestments is due, prevented the clergy from following the example of the laity, and left the cassock as the distinctive outer garment of the clergy on ordinary occasions, as it still remains. The dignity attaching to a long garment was also probably a factor in causing its ecclesiastical retention.

The Eucharistic vestments were placed over the cassock, as the cassock was placed over the undergarments of the wearer. But it was so entirely concealed by the long alb that it could scarcely be regarded as an essential part of the vestments for the Eucharistic office. The case was different,

History of the Processional Vestments. 139

however, when the priest was vested in processional attire, for the lower end of the cassock appeared very prominently under the surplice, and its presence was consequently essential to complete the processional outfit. We therefore discuss this vestment under the head 'Processional' rather than under the head 'Eucharistic.'

Cassocks were originally invented for purposes of warmth, and hence were lined with furs. This custom was retained when the cassock became exclusively a clerical dress, and we often find in monuments of ecclesiastics indications at the wrist that the cassock was so lined. The colour of the vestment was invariably black for ordinary ecclesiastics, scarlet for doctors of divinity and cardinals, purple for bishops and prelates, and on high occasions for acolytes; for the Pope, white. The fur with which the cassock was lined was ermine or some other precious kind for dignitaries; but ordinary priests were strictly forbidden to wear anything more costly than sheepskin. The cassock as we find it represented on mediaeval monuments was probably open to the breast; I do not recollect having observed any counterpart to the modern cassock, with a row of buttons from neck to hem (humorously compared by Lord Grimthorpe to a boiler with a close row of rivets!). In some parts of France and in Rome the cassock is kept in place by a sash; this also is a modern innovation probably suggested by the custom of members of the monastic orders.

II. *The Surplice.* — From its fur lining, the cassock was called in mediaeval Latin the *pellicea*; the name *superpellicea* was accordingly given to the vestment which was worn immediately over it —a name which has passed by natural phonetic modifications into 'surplice.'

It will be remembered that the *alba* of the second or transitional epoch was a very much more ample vestment than its successor in mediaeval times. The chasuble, tunicle, or dalmatic (sometimes all three) had to be put on over it—an impossibility if it had maintained its original size. It accordingly was contracted in size in order to adapt itself to the new requirements; but in so doing the needleworkers went to the other extreme, and produced a vestment which threatened to become intractable every time the attempt was made to put it on over the cassock when the latter article of dress was thick and lined with fur. These difficulties resulted in the invention of a new garment, which retained the amplitude of the old *alba*, and was worn only when no vestment of importance (except the cope, which was adaptable) was put on over it. This was the surplice. The alb was retained for the Eucharistic service, as the upper vestments would lie over it more conveniently.

History of the Processional Vestments. 141

The surplice was a sleeved vestment of white linen, plain, except at the neck, where there was occasionally a little embroidery in coloured threads. The sleeves were very full, and hung down to a considerable length when the hands were conjoined, as they generally are in monuments. The surplice was put on by being passed over the head, exactly like the alb; the modern surplice, open in front, and secured at the neck with a button, was invented within the last two hundred years, and was designed to make the assumption of the vestment possible without disarranging the enormous wigs which were worn during the seventeenth and eighteenth centuries.

III. *The Rochet* is a still further modification of the alb. The sleeves are reduced to a minimum or totally absent. It appears to have been worn, though not always, by choristers, and there is also evidence that it was the form of surplice favoured by bishops. Thus we read:

'Item 8 surplices for the quere.

'Item 3 rochets *for children.*'—Inventory of St Mary Hill, London.

'Bis adiit [Richardus de Bury] summum pontificem Johannem et recepit ab eo rochetam in loco bullae pro proximo episcopatu vacante ex post in Anglia.'—Will. de Chambre, 'Continuatio Hist. Dunelmensis,' Surtees Society, 1839, p. 127.

IV. *The Cotta.*—This is a surplice, considerably modified, which has the advantage of being cheap, and is accordingly worn as a substitute for the longer surplice in poor parishes. It is a sleeveless vestment, of crochet work or crimped linen, which reaches to the middle of the back. It has not an effective appearance.

V. *The Almuce,** which is also variously styled the Amys, or Amess,† was a hood lined with fur, and, like the cassock, designed to protect the priest from cold. In winter-time the churches— never very warm—would have been uninhabitable before the invention of heating stoves, had it not been for comforting articles of apparel such as these.

It was shaped so that it could lie over the shoulders as a tippet, or be drawn over the head as a hood, and it must have been very necessary during the protracted services of the middle ages. The vestment was almost always of black cloth, as was the cassock; and the fur with which it was lined varied in quality and colour with the degree of the wearer. Doctors of divinity and canons wore an almuce lined with gray fur, the former

---

* This word is a curious hybrid. The *muce* is the Teutonic for a cap or hood (*cf.* Scottish *mutch*, German *Mütze*). The word *mozetta* is connected with this. The *al* is the Arabic article, probably attached to it at some time in Spain.

† Both objectionable terms, as they lead to confusion with the *amice*, the sound of all these words being practically indistinguishable.

being further distinguished from the latter by the scarlet colour of the outside cloth; all others wore ordinary dark brown fur. A singular embellishment of this vestment consisted in the addition of the tails of the animals from which the fur lining was taken sewn round the border of the vestment.

At about the year 1300 the almuce, as a hood, was superseded by a cap, which will be described in its proper place. It was therefore thrown back, and suffered to fall behind, somewhat after the fashion of the hood worn in our modern universities. In order to prevent it from slipping off when in this position, it was sewn in front, so that an aperture was made through which the head of the wearer had to be passed. During the fourteenth century it gradually almost entirely lost its hood shape, and became more and more like a tippet, the only relic of its original form being the two long tails which hung in front somewhat like the ends of a stole, and which were doubtless the remains of the strings with which the original hood was fastened. The row of 'cattes tayles' (as the Elizabethan reformers called them) was also retained.

When the almuce was in position on the head, the fur was inside, the cloth outside. Obviously, when the vestment was thrown back over the shoulder, the fur would be outside, the cloth inside. This is a perfectly natural and intelligible transformation. Mrs Dolby, in noticing it, speaks of it in a most misleading manner. After describing the various changes which it underwent from hood to tippet, she says, 'By this time, too, what was originally the outside of the garment had become the lining, and the fur the only material rendered visible,' as though some ecclesiastical ordinance or the freak of some clerical tailor had brought about this transformation. And Dr Rock says: 'Not the least remarkable thing in these changes of the "furred amys" [as he calls it] is, that it became, as it were, turned inside out.' The remarkable thing would have been if anything else had happened.

At Wells Cathedral is the monument of Dean Huse (*ob.* 1305, but the tomb is a century and half later), on which are sculptured, besides the principal effigy, a series of small figures of canons holding books. The almuces of these figures show a unique peculiarity : the tails are fastened together on the breast by a cord which passes through them and hangs down with tasselled ends.

Mr St John Hope, in a paper in 'Archaeologia,' vol. liv, p. 81, has traced the history of the appearance of the almuce during the thirteenth and fourteenth centuries by reference to sculptured effigies and brasses in England. From this paper I extract the following illustrative examples :

History of the Processional Vestments. 145

1. An effigy in Hereford Cathedral, *circa* 1311, shows the almuce 'like a short cape down to the elbows, with long and broad pendants in front, and turned back round the neck like a loose, high-standing collar. The chief point to notice, however, is that the vestment is quite open in front and not joined on the breast, showing that it was put on like a woman's shawl.'

2. Another effigy in the same cathedral, *circa* 1320, shows a similar arrangement with the addition of a large morse to fasten the almuce.

3. In the fifteenth century, when the pendent tails became common, we find two brasses at Cobham, Kent, one showing the almuce clasped on the breast by a brooch, the other showing it open all down the front under the cope.

4. In a drawing at New College, Oxford, executed about 1446, the Warden of Winchester College is represented in a furred almuce not open in front, but the Fellows who stand near him wear almuces laced up the front. This drawing is reproduced in 'Archaeologia,' vol. liii, plate 14.

5. An effigy dating from the very end of the fifteenth century in St Martin's, Birmingham, illustrates the almuce as it appeared when the cape was joined completely across the breast.

To these facts we may add that as a general rule the two front tails in the earlier representations of almuces have plain ends; in those of later representations (from *circa* 1450) the tails have a small ornamental tassel, or tuft, attached to their ends.

VI. *The Cope.*—The cope may date back, as a vestment, to the ninth century, but in that form it is certainly not older. Before that time it was nothing more or less than an overcoat, which the clergy kept on in their cold and draughty churches or in open-air processions. It is represented in an Anglo-Saxon pontifical of *circa* 900 as a plain cloth vestment, fastened at the neck by a brooch or morse; the shape is similar to that which we find in later times. The shape of the cope was very much that of half the chasuble. It was secured at the neck by a brooch, and suffered to drape on the person.

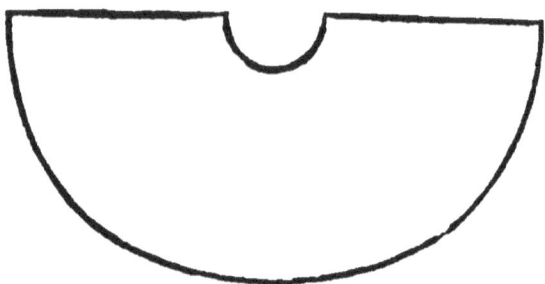

The material, at least in mediaeval times, was silk, cloth of gold, velvet, or other precious stuffs. It was magnificently embroidered, jewelled, and enriched with precious metals, the embroideries consisting either of strips along the straight edges, which hung down in front, or else of these strips

History of the Processional Vestments. 147

combined with patterns running over the entire surface of the vestment, or confined to the lower border. It is hard to say whether the cope or the chasuble was the richer vestment in the fourteenth and fifteenth centuries.

The cope, being originally a costume for outdoor processions, was furnished with a hood at the back; but when the almuce took its place, it degenerated, like so many other vestments, or parts of vestments, into a mere ornamental appendage; it lost its hood form (which would somewhat have interfered with the appearance of the almuce) and became a triangular flap, usually embroidered with some scene in sacred or legendary history. In many copes these hoods were absent, while to others there were several hoods, so that subjects appropriate to the day could be hooked on. This triangular flap gradually assumed curvilinear sides, till ultimately the angle disappeared altogether and the flap became semicircular.

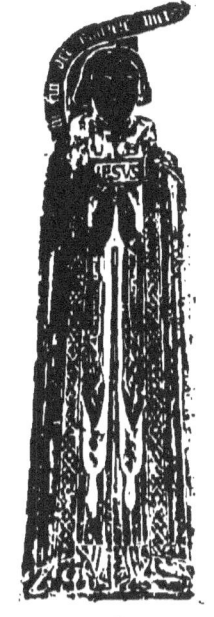

FIG. 19. — BRASS OF ARCHDEACON MAGNUS, SESSAY, YORKSHIRE, 1550 (showing Processional vestments, including hooded cope).

The 'morse,' or brooch, with which the cope was fastened, was the counterpart of the rational.

It was made of gold or of silver, or else of wood overlaid with one of these metals. It was often enamelled and jewelled, and was of a great variety of shapes.

VII. *The Canon's Cope.*—This vestment must be carefully distinguished from the *cappa serica*, or ordinary cope. It was a simple choir robe, worn at ordinary services, of black cloth, permanently sewn at the neck, though open from the breast downwards, so that it had to be passed over the head. It was not ornamented in any way, and probably for this reason was not popular as an object for treatment among manuscript illuminators or monument sculptors and engravers. A hood was appended, which usually hung on the back.

VIII. *The Mozetta.*—This is a cape worn over the cope by the Pope, cardinals, and bishops in the Roman Church. It is of white fur or coloured silk, according to the season ; the Pope wears a red mozetta bordered with ermine when holding receptions ; canons in choir wear a black, bishops and (on penitential seasons) cardinals a violet mozetta ; on ordinary occasions cardinals wear a mozetta of red. The vestment is probably a descendant of the almuce, and kin to the *chimere*.

IX. *The Roman Collar.*—This being an entirely modern vestment, is properly outside our range. It is an embroidered imitation of the turndown shirt-collar of ordinary dress.

In mediaeval monuments the throat of the priest is exposed, as are also those of present-day members of the older religious orders. Considerations of comfort and appearance have led to the adoption of this collar for the ordinary clergy. It should be 'made,' says Mrs. Dolby, 'of a perfectly straight piece of fine linen or lawn,' and 'bordered on the turnover side and along its short ends by a neatly-stitched hem of hálf an inch. Opened out, when made, it is two and three-quarter inches wide ; the turndown should be not more than one and a half inch deep. . . . The Roman collar worn by a bishop is violet, that of a cardinal is scarlet.'

X. *Ecclesiastical Head-dress.*—Pseudo-Alcuin expressly contrasts the Churches of the East and West in this—that the Western clergy officiated at the mass bareheaded, which was not the practice of those of the Eastern Church. This gives us information as to the usage of the Western Church at about the tenth or twelfth century. In the following century a cap is noticed 'as one of the marks by which a Churchman might be known';[*] and it appears in inventories, classed along with mitres.

The use of a cap at Divine service was a matter of special papal permission : thus, Innocent IV issued an indult in 1245 to the Prior and Convent

[*] Rock.

Ecclesiastical Vestments.

of St Andrew's, Rochester, permitting them to wear caps (*pileis uti*) in the choir, provided that due reverence be observed at the gospel and the elevation. Two forms of cap are to be seen in mediaeval monuments: one a simple dome-shaped skull-cap, called *birettum*; the other a circular cap, with a point in the centre, of this shape ⌒, which was peculiar to university dignitaries. The latter is probably the ancestor of the modern *biretta*; and, indeed, in a brass of Robert Brassie in King's College Chapel, Cambridge (1558), appears a head-dress which is a connecting link between the two.

The head-dress was always black, except for cardinals and a few bishops and others to whom the privileges of cardinals had been especially granted. These wore scarlet.

We have reserved for the conclusion of this chapter a more detailed account of the subjects with which, and the manner in which these various articles of sacred apparel were decorated.

FIG. 20.—BRASS OF ROBERT BRASSIE, KING'S COLLEGE, CAMBRIDGE (showing almuce and biretta-like cap).

Vestments, as represented in mediaeval sculptures or illuminations, the testimony of which is con-

History of the Processional Vestments. 151

firmed by the examples which actually exist, are not as a general rule ornamented in a haphazard manner over the whole surface. The ornamentation is usually concentrated into patches of embroidery or jewel-work, which are sewn on to certain definite places in the vestment.

In describing the vestments singly we have already noticed the positions in which these patches of embroidery were placed. It will be convenient, however, to bring all these particulars together and briefly remind the reader of them.

The *alb* was decorated with a rectangular patch on the breast; another on the back; two more above the lower hem, one in front, one behind; a small patch on each cuff (entirely encircling the wrist in older examples); and a narrow binding round the neck. The patches on the hem were sometimes suspended loose from the belt, and the patches on the breast and back fastened together and suspended loose over the shoulders.

The *amice* was decorated with a band of embroidery along one side, which was practically the only part of the vestment visible when it was in position.

The *stole* and *maniple* were embroidered along their whole length; they usually ended in a rectangular or trapezium-shaped piece of cloth, embroidered with a different pattern from that which ornamented the rest of the vestment (usually some form of cross), and fringed along its lower border.

The *dalmatic*, besides the peculiar arrangement of fringes already described, was ornamented with a series of horizontal bands of embroidered work, running right across the body of the vestment. The *bishop's dalmatic* was usually embroidered all over.

The *chasuble* was almost invariably adorned with an edging of embroidered work, and when the body of the vestment was adorned it was usually with some of the many modifications of the ⲯ or Y cross.

The *sandals* were sometimes ornamented all over, sometimes decorated with a ⲯ cross, the upper part of the cross being turned towards the toe.

The *pall* properly had no ornamentation except its crosses.

The *stockings* were either not embroidered at all or richly embroidered over the whole surface.

The *rational* was decorated with enamel, goldsmith's or jewelled work.

The *mitra simplex* was decorated with little or no adornment; the *mitra aurifrigiata* with embroidered work all over it; the *mitra pretiosa* with embroidery combined with jewels and goldsmith's work.

The *gloves* do not appear to have been con-

History of the Processional Vestments. 153

spicuously ornamented. They often bore a large jewel set against the back of the hand.

The *tunicle* was generally quite simple; the *bishop's tunicle*, however, in no wise differed from the dalmatic.

Of the *orale* a full description has already been given; we need not again refer to it.

Passing to the Processional and other vestments, it will be unnecessary to mention any but the *cope*; for, with the exception of a little trifling embroidered work in coloured threads round the neck of the surplice, none of the other vestments showed any ornamentation. The cope was ornamented with embroidered work down the straight edges in front, and often round the bottom edge and the neck as well; often also the whole vestment was elaborately embroidered all over. The hood, too, must not be forgotten.

For some inscrutable reason a distinction is drawn in name between the embroidered ornaments of the alb and amice and those of the remainder of the ecclesiastical dress. The former are called apparels, the latter orphreys.

The subjects with which these vestments are embroidered must next engage our attention for a short time. These fall naturally into three broad groups :

1. Conventional and meaningless devices.
2. Symbols or figures of Divine or beatified

persons, or passages of Scripture and other religious inscriptions.

3. Personal devices.

The number of conventional patterns which meet us embroidered on ecclesiastical vestments is endless, and to attempt to catalogue even the most striking would be an undertaking the magnitude of which would only be equalled by its uselessness. A small collection of rubbings of monumental brasses will convince the reader of this. Floral devices are the most common, either in continuous scrolls or in repetitions and variations of the same pattern ; and these are found combined with patterns of the other two groups to fill up the gaps and spandrels between different figures or letters. But grotesque and real animals, wild men, and various other objects of natural history, all have their place; though, if the evidence of the monuments be reliable, these were not so common in England as in the other countries which yielded allegiance to the Western Church. It is, of course, possible that some of these figures may have been intended as emblems of saints,* and others may have been heraldic ; but it is probable

---

* For example, the lamb (besides its more sacred significance) may possibly be taken as symbolical of St Agnes, the dragon of St George or St Margaret, the lion of St Jerome, the lily, sun, moon, stars, or rose of St Mary the Virgin, and so on indefinitely.

that the majority of them were simply ornaments with no other intention beyond filling up space effectively.

The symbols of Divine or beatified persons are of more interest. These are usually found on the centre orphreys of the chasuble, on the edges and hood of the cope, on mitres, and on rationals or morses, the orphreys of the other vestments being usually conventional, floral, or animal devices. The hood of the cope almost invariably bore some emblematic or sacred device, or else some scene in sacred or traditional history; the edge of the cope and the centre of the chasuble often bore figures of saints in niches, one above another, or else connected scenes from the life of a saint; while the rationals and morses, which were under the province of the enamellers (and were consequently more easily decorated than the embroidered vestments), usually displayed some more elaborate design in miniature.

Of the greatest importance, however, are devices of the third order—those which display the name, initials, rebus, or coat-of-arms of the wearer or the donor of the vestment. In monuments these designs invariably are connected with the name and family of the wearer, while the personal devices recorded in inventories are usually connected with the donor. The reason is, probably, that the vestments catalogued in inventories originally were made for, and worn by, the donors thereof; during their lifetime the devices showed forth the wearers' names; after their death, the names of the testators: while the monuments, which were supposed as nearly as possible to represent the persons commemorated as they appeared while they lived, would naturally pourtray the vestments which they wore, or might have worn, when celebrating mass or conducting the other offices of church service.

Mediaeval priests and embroiderers seem to have shrunk from placing these personal devices on the chasuble, though such ornamentation is not altogether unknown even in that most reverenced of vestments. Thus, at Arundel, Sussex, is a brass representing a priest in ecclesiastic vestments, in which the initials of the wearer occur on the chasuble. The cope, however, often shows initials or other designs* which serve to identify

* Examples of an entire name occurring on copes are extremely rare. I only know of one—the brass of Thomas Patesley (1418), at Great Shelford, Cambridgeshire. Initials are common in almost every county; *rebuses* not quite so common, though we have the famous *maple*-leaves (alternating with *M*'s) in the cope of a priest called Mapleton, as shown on his brass at Broadwater, Sussex; while heraldic devices are fairly frequent, either as complete shields or selections from the charges borne by the priest's family. The brasses of Wm. de Fulbourne, at Fulbourne, Cambridgeshire, and of Thos. Aileward, at Havant, Hampshire, give us examples of both these methods of ornamentation.

the wearer. The same chariness does not seem to have been felt with regard to the other Eucharistic vestments, possibly because they were not so exclusively appropriated to the Eucharistic service. Thus, at Beverley Minster there is a sculptured effigy of a priest whose entire stole is covered with a series of coats-of-arms.

As I have already said, this group of orphrey patterns is of considerably greater importance than the other two, which cannot be regarded as other than mere artistic curiosities. It is generally possible to identify the personality of the priest commemorated by a monument, even if the inscription be lost or defaced, when these convenient symbols enter into the composition of the orphreys on his vesture. This helps us in assigning the date of the monument; and every monument of which we know the date exactly adds something to our stock of knowledge respecting the chronology of mediæval art.

As giving an idea of the number and variety of the designs employed by the embroiderers and enamellers to decorate the vestments of the church, it has been thought that the following table will not be found uninteresting. It is a classified catalogue of the designs enumerated in a single inventory of a single collection of vestments, the inventory of the commissioners of Henry VIII, drawn up in 1536, of the property of Lincoln Cathedral.

Ecclesiastical Vestments.

It has not been considered necessary to preserve the uncouth spelling of the original, especially as some words are scarcely spelt the same way twice in the course of the document. Nor has it been thought worth while to swell the bulk of the list by giving details as to the parts of the vestments on which the various objects are represented, or the frequency with which those occurring more than once are found, the purpose of the list being simply to show faintly the variety of designs at the disposal of the embroiderer or enameller. It should be premised that this is by no means a complete list; in many cases the inventory gives little or no information concerning the decoration of the vestment catalogued. Most probably, however, all ornaments of interest or importance are here included:

Group I

Flowers:
    Fleurs-de-lys (possibly heraldic).
    Roses,} possibly emblematic of St Mary the Virgin.
    Lilies,}

Birds and beasts, or parts thereof:
    Leopards.
    Harts.
    Falcons.
    Falcons bearing crowns of gold in their mouths (probably heraldic).
    Swans.
    Ostriches.

Ostrich feathers.
Popinjays.
Lions.
Owls.
Black eagles.
Peacocks.
Gryphons.
Dragons.
Phœnix.

Miscellaneous:
Knots.
Clouds.
Crowns.
(Also a few others, properly included under Group II.)

Group II

Divine Persons:
The Holy Trinity.
Our Lord.
The Majesty.
The Holy Ghost, Crucifix, and St Mary the Virgin.

Incidents in the life of Our Lord, and His emblems:
Our Lord with the Cross.
The Passion, in scenes.
The Crucifixion.
Ditto, with SS Mary and John on either side.
Ditto, ditto, the Father above.
The Ascension.
Our Lord sitting on the rainbow.
The root of Jesse.
The vernacle.
The Holy Lamb.
Crosses.

Members of the Holy Host of Heaven:
[Archangels, angels, and images, passim.]
Two angels singing.
Two angels incensing.
An angel bearing a crown.
Two angels bearing St John Baptist's head (properly heraldic).
An angel with a harp.
Scenes in the life of St Mary the Virgin and her emblems:
Salutation.
St Mary; on the left side three kings, on the right two shepherds, and an angel with 'Gloria in excelsis.'
St Mary with the Holy Child.
Ditto, and St Mary Magdalene.
Burial.
Assumption.
Coronation.
'Our lady of pity.'
Wm. Marshall (donor of vestment) kneeling to the Virgin.
Suns, Moons, Stars.
Roses, lilies. (See Group I.)
Other Saints and their emblems:
'History of Apostles and Martyrs.'
St Peter.
St Catherine.
St Catherine (the tomb springing oil).
St John Baptist.
St Bartholomew.
History of St John Baptist, ⎫ Probably in different
History of St Thomas,   ⎭ scenes.
Wheels (St Catherine).
Keys (St Peter).
The Majesty, SS Mary the Virgin, Peter, Paul, the four evangelists, and a man kneeling to them.

History of the Processional Vestments. 161

Various Scenes in Sacred History:
Eve eating of the tree.
The massacre of the innocents.
The last judgment.

Uncertain and Miscellaneous Subjects:
A bishop (probably some saint).
A king (perhaps King David).
Kings and prophets.
Two kings crowned.

Inscriptions:
The hye wey ys best.
'Divers verses.'
Da gloriam deo.
Gracia dei sum, etc.
Vox domini super aquas.
Cena dñi.

Also the following, which form a connecting-link between the second and third groups, being requests for prayers for the donors of vestments:

Orate pro anima Magistri Willelmi Skelton.
„   „   Willelmi Spenser capellani.
„   „   Magistri Ricardi Smyth vycar de Worseworth.
„   „   Roberti Dercy.
Memoriale Willelmi Marshall olim virgarii hujus ecclesiae.

GROUP III

Heraldic:
Leopards powdered with black trefoils (? leopards ermine).
'White harts crowned with chains on their necks full of these letters S.S.'

Ecclesiastical Vestments.

Orphreys with diverse arms.
Mullets.
'All may God amend' (Rudyng motto), together with Rudyng arms and badges.
'A shield paled.'
Arms of Lord Chadworth.

Names, Initials, and Dedicatory Inscriptions:
Ricūs de Gravesend.
T.S., I.C., O.L., P.D. (on different vestments).
Ex dono Johannis Reed Capellani Cantar' quondam cantarie Ricardi Whitwell.
Southam ex dono Johannis Southam.
Ex dono M^{ri} Willelmi Smyth archidiaconi Lincoln.

In many vestments, especially among those of early date, the embroidery is of a distinctly Oriental character, which, if not actually Byzantine, is founded on Byzantine models. These were popularized throughout Europe by the Mohammedan weavers and their successors of the royal establishment in Sicily. Often vestments are found bearing Arabic or other Oriental inscriptions; these are sometimes meaningless, like the patterns formed with Arabic letters on many Eastern shawls and cloths of modern times, but occasionally they give important information as to the date and origin of the vestment which they decorate. The coronation vestments of the German Emperors, now at Vienna, are of entirely Eastern character, and the cope bears inscriptions in Cufic characters, telling us that it was made at Palermo

History of the Processional Vestments. 163

in 1133. Occasionally the Eastern ornaments and inscriptions are *forged* (alas, for mediaeval morality!), in order to counterfeit the workmanship of the highly popular Eastern looms. Sometimes we find clumsy imitations of Arabic words treated ignorantly by the forger as ornaments, the word being written correctly, though in an obviously amateurish manner, from right to left, and a replica *reversed* set opposite to it, in order to balance it symmetrically!

No country excelled England in embroidered work in the middle ages. Matthew Paris's story of Pope Innocent IV's admiration of some English vestments is well known. His holiness, 'seeing some desirable orphreys in the copes and *infulae* of certain English ecclesiastics, asked where they had been made. "In England," was the answer. "Truly is England our garden of delights," said he; "truly is it a well inexhaustible; and where much is, thence can much be extorted." Whereupon the Pope, allured by the lust of the eyes, sent his sealed letters to nearly all the abbots of the Cistercian order in England (to whose prayers he had just been committing himself in the chapter-house of the Cistercian order) that they should not delay to send those orphreys to himself—getting them for nothing, if possible—to decorate his chasubles and choral copes.' Matthew Paris concludes his narrative by telling us that the

London merchants were gratified enough, but that many were highly offended at the open avarice of the Head of the Church.*

This leads us to another point to be noticed with regard to mediaeval vestments—their value as articles of merchandise. In the 'Issues of the Exchequer,' 24, 25 Henry III (A.D. 1241-1242), there are several entries of expenses involved in purchasing vestments. Thus we find 4l. 19s. paid to Adam de Basinges 'for a gold cope purchased by our command and placed in our chapel at the feast of the Nativity of our Lord in the 25th year of our reign : also to the same 24l. 1s. 6d. for a cope of red silk given to the Bishop of Hereford by our command in the same year and day : also

* Eisdemque diebus dominus papa videns in aliquorum Anglicorum ornamentis ecclesiasticis, utpote in capis choralibus et infulis aurifrisia concupiscibilia, interrogavit ubinam facta puissent. Cui responsum est In Anglia. At ipse, Vere hortus noster deliciarum est Anglia ; vere puteus inexhaustus est ; et ubi multa abundant de multis multa possunt extorqueri. Unde idem dominus papa concupiscentia illectus oculorum literas suas bullatas sacras misit ad omnes fere Cisterciensis ordinis abbates in Anglia commorantes quorum orationibus se nuper in capitulo Cisterciensi commendaverat ut ipsi aurifrisia ac si pro nihilo ipsa possent adquirere mittere non different praecelecta ad planetas et capas suas chorales adomandas. Quod mercennariis Londoniae qui ea venalia habebant non displicuit, ad placitum vendentibus : unde multi manifestum avaritiam Romanae ecclesiae detestabantur.— M. Paris, 'Chronica Majora' (Rolls Series), vol. iv, p. 546.

History of the Processional Vestments. 165

to the same 17l. 18s. 10d. for two diapered and one precious cloth of gold, for a tunic and dalmatican entirely ornamented with gold fringe purchased by our command and placed in our chapel the same year and day : also to the same 47s. 10d. for a chesable of silk cloth without gold purchased by our command and placed in our chapel : also to the same 7s. 2d. for an albe embroidered with gold fringe purchased by our command and placed in our chapel: also to the same 17l. 1 mark for two embroidered chesables purchased by our command and placed in our chapel.'* The same year the enormous sum of £82 was given by the King for a mitre.

It has been calculated that the present value of money is fifteen times greater than it was in the thirteenth century. Applying this principle, we obtain the following results, which give a clearer idea of the value of the vestments purchased by the King:

A cope costing 4l. 19s. would be worth, at present rates, £74 5s.

A cope costing 24l. 1s. 6d. would be worth, at present rates, £361 2s. 6d.

Tunic and dalmatic costing 17l. 18s. 10d. would be worth, at present rates, £269 2s. 6d.

A chasuble costing 2l. 7s. 10d. would be worth, at present rates, £35 17s. 6d.

---

* 'Issues of the Exchequer' (ed. Dover), p. 16.

An alb costing 7s. 2d. would be worth, at present rates, £5 7s. 6d.

Two chasubles costing 17l. 13s. 4d. would be worth, at present rates, £265.

A mitre costing 82l. would be worth, at present rates, £1,230.

Even if we allow that these vestments, being royal gifts, or royal furniture, were of larger price than usual, it still remains evident that a set of vestments was an expensive luxury. And when we consider the enormous number of vestments which were existing in the different cathedral establishments, we can hardly wonder at the cupidity of Henry VIII being aroused. Mr St John Hope has calculated that in Lincoln (of which we possess perhaps the fullest set of inventories) the commissioners of 1536 found 125 red copes, 7 purple, 20 green, 36 blue, 9 black, 60 white, 2 yellow, 2 various, and perhaps 4 for choristers—265 in all; 16 red chasubles, 3 purple, 6 green, 11 blue, 5 black, 9 white, 1 yellow and 1 various—52 in all; 2 dalmatics, 94 tunicles, and 131 albs, not to mention other property in embroidered work, such as altar frontals, or in precious metal, such as chalices. It is, of course, impossible to assign an estimate of the value of this vestry, but even if we reckoned the copes at £50 of our money—a low estimate in the majority of cases—these vestments alone would

History of the Processional Vestments. 167

be worth £13,250 together. But this is pure guesswork and of no practical value ; of more importance is such an entry as the following, from the old Durham 'Book of Rites' (printed by the Surtees Society) :

'*Prossession of Hallowe Thursdaie, Whitsondaie & Trinitie Sonday, by the Prior and the Monnckes.*—The next morninge, being Hallow Thursdaie, they had also a generall Prossession, with two crosses borne before theme, the one of the crosses, the staff and all, of gould, the other of sylver and parcell gilt . . . with all the riche Copes that was in the Church, every Monnke had one, and the Prior had a marvellous riche cope on, of clothe of ffyne pure gould, the which he was not able to goe upright with it, for the weightines thereof, but as men did staye it and holde it up of every side when he had it on. He went with his crutch in his hand, which was of sylver and duble gilt, with a rich myter on his head.'

In the private account-book of the last prior but one of Worcester* is given the following interesting bill for a mitre :

'Item to John Cranckes gold smyth of london for al maner of stuff belongyng of the new mytur, with the makyng of the same as hit apereth by parcelles foloyng :
In primis for v grete stones - - - xvis viijd.
Item for ᪲iiij & vj stones prece viijd apeece to
  the frontes - - ◆ - - - lvijs iiijd.
Item for xxj stones sett in golde, weyng di.
  vnces - - - - - - - xiijs iiijd.
Item for xl medyll stones, prece vjd a stone xxs.

---

* Quoted in the *Builder*, 7 July 1894.

Item for ᵘⁱⁱⱼ & xv smale stones prece iiijd a
stone, to garnesshe - - - - - xxvs.
Item for iij vnces & a quarter of fyne peerll,
at iij li. the vnce - - - - - iij* li xvs.
Item for xij vnces of medull peerll, at xs the
vnce - - - - - - - vj li.
Item the selver warke weys, in all ᵘⁱⁱⱼ xiij vnces,
which is with the fassheon & all - - xxiiij li xvjs.
Item to the broderar vj wokes (? *wekes*) xijd
a day, besydes mete & dryncke - - xxxvjs.
Item payd for lynnen cloth to cowech ytt on
with perll - - - - - - vijd.
Item for sylke to thred the seid perll & steche
the peerll j vnce & di - - - - xvd.
Item for yalow thred - - - - - jd.
Item for Rybande of iiijd brede ij yeards - viijd.
Item for Reband of ijd brede A yearde - ijd.
Item for Rownde selk about the bordure - jd. ob.
Item for red selke to sow hytt with all, di.
quarter the vnce - - - - - ijd ob.
Item for past - - - - - - iiijd.
(Item) for a quarter of sarcenett to lyne hytt xiiijd.
Item for a case to the mytur of lethur - - iiijs.
Summa xlixli. xvs. the coste of the mytur.'

Before parting with the ancient vestments of the Western Church, let us spend a few moments on another, and to the antiquary a melancholy, subject, namely, the fate which has befallen them. The number of actual vestments which survive to our own day is comparatively small. Notwithstanding the scrupulous care with which they were

* *Sic.*, should be viiij or ix.

kept, the action of time and probably of moths could not but destroy the perishable material of which they were made; and as so sacred were they regarded that when a vestment was worn out it was burnt, and the ashes thrown into and washed down the drain of the piscina, or font; so, at least, it was ordered by the ninth canon of the Synod of Dublin, 1186.* In France and in England, however, far the greatest havoc was wrought in the religious and political troubles of the eighteenth century in the former case, of the two centuries preceding in the latter.

The destruction of churches and church property in France at the hands of the atheistical mobs of the Revolution was incalculable. Monuments, glass and fabrics were broken and ruined, if not utterly destroyed, and the vestments and Processional crosses were torn from the treasuries and heaped up in the streets to be burnt in bonfires. In England the damage was perhaps even more considerable, though it was executed in a quieter and more deliberate manner. In the reaction after the revival of the Roman faith under Queen Mary, orders were sent to the churchwardens of the different parishes requesting returns from them as to the relics of popery, if any, which remained in the churches under their care, and the manner

* Worn-out vestments were also found useful for the interment of ecclesiastics, as we have seen, supra p. 101.

in which such superstitious objects had been disposed of, whenever they had been removed. A very perfect series of these returns exists for Lincolnshire, and they have been edited by Mr Edward Peacock, F.S.A., in a highly-interesting volume entitled 'English Church Furniture and Decorations,' published in 1866. In each return is a note describing what was done with the vestments and other pre-Reformation furniture of the church to which the return relates. From them we extract the following entries, which may serve as specimens of the varied fate of vestments, not only in the county of Lincoln, but throughout the country :

Alford. Itm̄ one cope whearof is made a clothe for the coīon table [a frequent entry].

Itm̄ one vestment [chasuble] sold and defacid [a frequent entry].

Ashbie iuxa Sleford. Itm̄ vestmētes copes crosses aulbes phanelles crosse clothes banner clothes and all such lyke ymplements—stollē out of or churche in quene maries tyme.

Ashbie iuxa Spillisbie. Itm̄ one vestm̄t with crose clothes —geven to the poore Aō iij° Regine Elizabth [a frequent entry].

Itm̄ an alb—whearof wee have made a surples [a frequent entry].

Aswardbie. Itm̄ two vestmentes were cut in peces yesterdaie and sold to Thomas waite and george holmes and the' haue put them to prophane vse.

Bomnbie. Itm̄ a vestm' and yē rest as fanells, stooles and such like—brent iiij yeare ago p̄te of the same and the rest hath made quishwines of John Michill and James Totter then churchwarden.

So we find at Braceby an alb made a covering for the font. At Castlebytham we find 'one cope one vestment and one albe' were 'sold to Thomas Inma' for the some of Vs. Vpon sondaie was a sevenighte wc̄h he haith defaced and cutt in peces.' Elsewhere, a vestment was made into a 'dublett,' others into 'clowtes for children,' or 'hangings for a bedd.' Some churches had lost their vestments in the Edwardian Reformation, and consequently, when they were required again in Queen Mary's reign, substitutes had to be borrowed from private owners. These were 'restored' to their possessors; in a few cases the churchwardens thoughtfully cut them in pieces before doing so.

There is one other series of vestments which deserves a passing notice—the vestments in which the newly-baptized were clothed. In the sixth or seventh century these consisted of the *alba*, the *sabanum*, the *chrismale*, and the *garland*. The alba was probably similar to the clerical alba; the form of the sabanum (σάβανον) is uncertain, but it was possibly not more than its name implies—simply a towel. The chrismale was a piece of white linen tied on the head, intended to keep the chrism in its place during the week in which these vestments were worn. The garland was a chaplet of flowers with which the baptized were crowned after baptism.

There is a rite in the Armenian Church in

172   *Ecclesiastical Vestments.*

·which the priest twists two threads, one white and one red, lifts them up under the cross, and then lays them on the person to be baptized. The white and red is obviously symbolical of the mingled blood and water which flowed from our Lord's side, but there are obscure traces in early writers which seem to indicate that this observance was of more general acceptance, and that the present rite is a corruption of something quite different. Durandus, in the 'Rationale Div. Off.,' vi, c. 82, speaks of the alba of baptism having upon it a red band like a 'corona,' and elsewhere we find a combination of red and white mentioned in connection with the robes of the neophytes.

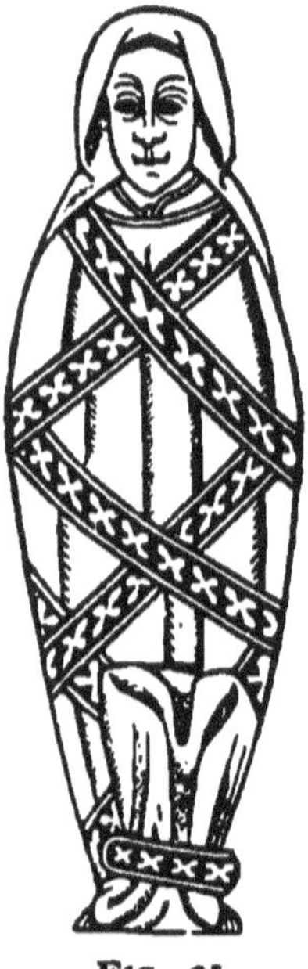

These vestments were worn throughout the week after baptism, and put off on the Sunday following, hence called *Dominica in albis depositis*. They were either retained after baptism as a memorial of the sacrament—and often used as shrouds after death—or else presented to the church by the baptized.

In the mediaeval church this comparatively elaborate suit was reduced to one cloth, the chrysome, or chrism cloth, in which the body of a newly-baptized infant

FIG. 21.

History of the Processional Vestments. 173

was swathed. This cloth was kept upon the child for a month, and if it died within the month the child was buried in it as a shroud. Several monumental brasses are extant in which children are represented in their baptismal robes; we reproduce an example in Chesham Bois Church, Buckinghamshire. In the modern Roman Church the white cloth is merely placed on the head; it is now too small to cover the body.

FIG. 22.—A COPE CHEST, YORK MINSTER.

The chrism cloth was taken off if the child survived till the end of the month, and returned to the church, in whose custody it was kept. These cloths were used for the reparation of vestments and altar hangings, and other sacred textile fabrics connected with the church. Thus in the Treasurer's Rolls for Ripon we read (1470-71) the following entries :

'Est de cc^ma lxvj vestibus crismalibus de reman. ultimi compoti praedicti. Et de c^ma iij vestibus crismalibus rec. de tot pueris baptizatis hoc anno. Summa ccciiij^xx ix.* De quibus.

'In sepultura puerorum viij. Et in reparacione vestimentorum, xiiij. Et liberantur pro manutergiis inde fiendis, ordinatis pro expensis ecclesiae, ix. Et liberantur pro calicibus involvendis et aliis necessariis ejusdem ecclesiae, vj. Summa xxxvij. Et reman. ccc^ma lij vestes crismales.'†

---

* There is an error of twenty somewhere in this calculation.

† 'Memorials of Ripon,' vol. iii, p. 219 (Surtees Society).

CHAPTER V.

THE VESTMENTS OF THE EASTERN CHURCHES.

THE proverbial conservatism of the unchanging East, which is felt in all ecclesiastical as well as in social matters, will make our task in the present chapter much lighter. The action of evolution, which makes the history of the Western vestments so complex, is hardly felt in the East. The mediaevalism, or, rather, primaevalism, which shuts out instrumental aid from the musical portions of the Eastern service acts upon vestments in minimizing the profusion of ornamentation which plays such an important part in the externals of Western ritual.

One of our earliest authorities on the subject of Eastern vesture is St Germanus of Constantinople (*circa* 715 A.D.). In his treatise Μυστικὴ Θεωρία he enters at considerable length into a discussion of Ecclesiastical Vestments and also of Monastic

Costume, giving details, which are curious, but of little or no value, concerning the alleged symbolic meanings which they bear.

In the present chapter we have to discuss the vestments of the principal Eastern Churches—the Orthodox 'Greek' Church, so called, the Armenian Church, and the remote body of Christians on the coast of Malabar. The general appearance and style of the vestments of these churches is similar; there are, however, minor differences, which will appear as we proceed.

The vestments and personal ornaments of the Orthodox Greek Church are as follows:

    I. The στοιχάριον.
   II. The ἐπιμανίκια.
  III. The ἐπιτραχήλιον.
  IV. The ὡράριον.
   V. The ζώνη.
  VI. The φαινόλιον.
 VII. The ἐπιγονάτιον.
VIII. The ὠμοφόριον.
  IX. The μάνδυας.
   X. The χαμαλαύχη.
  XI. The ἐξωχαμαλαύχη.
 XII. The πατέρεσσα.
XIII. The ἐγκόλπιον.
XIV. The σάκκος.

The Armenian vestments are as follows:

   I. The Vakass.
  II. The Shapich.
 III. The Poor-ourar.

The Vestments of the Eastern Churches. 177

IV. The Kodi.
V. The Pasbans.
VI. The Shoochar.
VII. The Sagavard.

FIG. 23.—ARMENIAN PRIEST.

The Malabar vestments are :

I. The Cuthino.
II. The Orro.
III. The Zunro.
IV. The Zando.
V. The Phaino.
VI. The Cap and Shoes.

I. The στοιχάριον was, and is, identical with the Roman *alba*. The word is of uncertain etymology, and none of the guesses which have been made are at all satisfactory. Like the *alba*, it was originally a garment of secular use ; this we infer

FIG. 24.—MALABAR PRIEST.

from the *Apologia contra Arianos*,* where we read that one charge (among others) which was brought against Athanasius was that he had required the Egyptians to furnish linen στοιχάρια. Germanus says of the vestment, ' being white, the στοιχάριον

* 'Patrol. Graec.,' xxv, 358.

FIG. 25.—DEACON IN στοιχάριον, ὠράριον, AND ἐπιμανίκια.

signifies the glory of the Godhead and the bright citizenship of priests. The stripes of the στοιχάριον on the sleeve signify the bonds of Christ; the stripes which run across signify the blood which flowed from Christ's side on the cross.' Setting aside the symbolism, we learn that the vestment in the time of Germanus was white, ornamented with stripes, probably red, upon the sleeves and across the body. At present, while the vestment is still white on ordinary occasions, on certain days coloured στοιχάρια are worn, as will be shown in the chapter on Ritual Use. The λωρία, or stripes, are now confined to the στοιχάρια of bishops. In Russia, and elsewhere to some extent, the στοιχάρια are often made of silk or velvet, though linen remains the proper material; here we see a notable correspondence with Western usage.

The *shapich* of the Armenians and the *cuthino* of the Malabar Christians correspond to this vestment and do not differ from it. It goes by other names in other parts of the Eastern Church; these are set forth in the appendix. Deacons, members of the minor orders, and choristers wear the shapich ungirded.

II. The ἐπιμανίκια. These correspond to the Western maniple, but they differ from it in several notable respects. First, one is provided for each arm instead of for the left arm only. Secondly, they are not worn pendant on the arm,

FIG. 26.—PRIEST IN στοιχάριον, ἐπιτραχήλιον, φαινόλιον, ζώνη, AND ἐπιμανίκια.

but are drawn round, so that they rather resemble cuffs than napkins suspended on the wrist. In some early mosaics they are shown not so much as cuffs, as large false sleeves. Something similar seems to have been worn in the Gallican Church, if we may accept the testimony of the MS. already referred to on p. 135.

This vestment—for the two pieces may be said technically to form one vestment—was for a long time restricted to bishops only, but priests and, since 1600, even deacons have had the right to wear it. Bishops only, however, are allowed to have the ἐπιμανίκια embroidered with the εἴκων of Christ.

The ἐπιμανίκια are alleged to signify the bands with which Christ was bound.

The Armenian *pasban* corresponds to the ἐπιμανίκιον; so does the *zando* of the Malabar Christians. Both *pasban* and *zando* are worn one on each wrist; but whereas the Armenian vestment is more like the Western maniple, the *zando* is a false sleeve, fitting the arm tightly and extending some way above the elbow.

III. The ἐπιτραχήλιον is in essence identical with the stole of the Western Church, but in form it differs widely. Instead of being a long narrow strip passed behind the neck, it is a short broad band with an aperture at one end, through which the wearer's head is passed, so that instead of two

FIG. 27.—ARCHIMANDRITE IN φαιρόλιον, ἐπιγονάτιον, ἐγκόλπιον, ETC.

ends pendant, one at each side, there is but one, hanging down in the middle. It is probably the richest of all the Eastern vestments; it is made of silk or brocade, and in large churches is ornamented with jewels and precious metals. A seam runs conspicuously down the middle, dividing the band into two; this gives the vestment a more stole-like appearance than it would otherwise possess.

The Armenian *poor-ourar* and the Malabar *orro* are the equivalents of this vestment, and resemble it in appearance. Both names are evidently corruptions of the Greek ὠράριον.

IV. The ὠράριον is the Diaconal substitute for the ἐπιτραχήλιον. It is identical with the Latin stole, and, like that vestment when worn by deacons, is carried on the left shoulder. St Germanus informs us that it typifies the ministry of angels, in that it resembles a pair of wings; this, like many other similar statements, may be taken for what it is worth. The sole difference between the ὠράριον and the stole lies in its ornamentation; the latter is ornamented in a perfectly unrestricted manner, the former bears embroidered upon it the τρισάγιον,

ΑΓΙΟΣ ΑΓΙΟΣ ΑΓΙΟΣ,

and the Armenian Church as a general rule dispenses even with this inscription.

FIG. 28.—BISHOP IN φαινόλιον, ἐπιγονάτιον, ὠμοφόριον, ETC.

V. The ζώνη is simply a girdle which keeps the στοιχάριον and ἐπιτραχήλιον in place. To it answers the Armenian *kodi* and the Malabar *zunro*. The Armenians suspend a large white napkin to the *kodi* on the left-hand side, which is used to wipe the hands or the vessels when necessary during the service, and thus takes the place of the old Western maniple.

VI. The φαινόλιον answers in all respects to the Western chasuble ; and it is evident that we are to see in its appellation the old name *paenula*. The Malabar Christians have a vestment called the *phaino*, which in appearance corresponds to the cope ; but its use assimilates it to the φαινόλιον, as we should expect from the identity of name. The *phaino* is made of more or less costly materials, it is square (not semicircular) in shape with rounded corners. A button and loop answer the purpose of the Western morse. It may be here stated that the embroidery and material of the *zando* usually corresponds with that of the *phaino* with which it is worn. The priests of the Armenian Church also wear a cope-shaped chasuble. Small bells are sometimes hung round the lower edge. The φαινόλιον of bishops was formerly distinguished from that of priests by being covered with crosses ; hence called φαινόλιον πολυσταύριον.

VII. The ἐπιγονάτιον is a lozenge-shaped ornament, made of brocade, and suspended by one corner on the right side of the ἐπιτραχήλια of bishops. It is ornamented with embroidery on its surface, and with tassels attached to the three free corners. It was originally a handkerchief, and it remained in this form for some considerable time; in fact, it remains a handkerchief in the Armenian Church. Although properly peculiar to bishops, certain other ecclesiastics wear it as a special privilege.

VIII. The ὠμοφόριον is equivalent to the Western *pall* (though it is worn by all prelates, not by archbishops only), and similar to it in shape; it is, however, rather wider, and is worn round the neck in a knot. It is said to symbolize the lost sheep — presumably from its being carried on the shoulder.

IX. The μάνδυας is a vestment similar to the cope, worn on certain occasions by Archimandrites and the higher orders of the Hierarchy. The difference between it and the Western cope consists in its being rather fuller, and fastened at the lower ends in front as well as at the top. Small bells are hung round its lower edge. The μάνδυας of an archimandrite is not ornamented; that of a prelate is decorated with wavy stripes called πόταμα καὶ πώματα, 'rivers and cups'*—a

* The assonance cannot be satisfactorily preserved in translation. Perhaps 'rivers and lavers' is the nearest approximation our language affords.

fanciful method of expressing the 'rivers of grace which flow from him.'*

X, XI. The χαμαλαύχη is a cap, the ἐξωχαμαλαύχη a hood worn over it. The ἐξωχαμαλαύχη of a Metropolitan is white, signed in front with a black cross, that of other prelates black.

XII. The πατέρισσα corresponds to the pastoral staff, but it is shorter and is used as an ordinary walking-stick, which it resembles in every particular. The handle is usually an ornamental modification of the crutched or tau cross. The bishops of the Eastern Church wear no ring.

XIII. The ἐγκόλπιον is a pectoral cross, worn in the East, and similar in all respects to the cross worn in the West.

XIV. The σάκκος is the equivalent of the Western dalmatic: it is now worn by all metropolitans.

The Armenian vestments which have not been described in the above conspectus are (i) the *sagavard*, or priest's cap ; (ii) the *vakass*, a vestment which corresponds to the Western amice, and is nowhere else worn in the East. It differs from it in the collar standing upright instead of being turned down. Attached to the *vakass* of high dignitaries is a breastplate of precious metals and stones, bearing the names of the twelve apostles. This is as obviously borrowed from the Jewish 'breastplate of the Ephod,' as the *vakass*

* Neale.

itself is borrowed from the Western amice; but the Armenians deny any Western influence in the dress, asserting the entire vestment to be of Jewish origin; (iii) the *shoochar*, which answers in every respect to the cope; and (iv) the sandals, which are worn during service, are kept in the church, and may not be used on other occasions.

Vartabeds (*i.e.*, priests especially entrusted with the work of preaching and instructing the ignorant in the principles of the religion) and bishops substitute a mitre for the *sagavard*, and wear a pectoral cross hanging by a gold chain round the neck. The copes of bishops are ornamented by two strips of brocade, usually embroidered with figures of saints; these are survivals of the *infulae* of the mitre, but are attached to the shoulder of the cope. Vartabeds are distinguished by a staff of which the head consists of a cross with two serpents turned round it.

The Armenian Church permits clergy to remain married if the marriage hath taken place before ordination. The ordinary dress of unmarried priests consists of a black or dark purple cassock with a broad belt, over which is worn a gown, and (at the recital of the offices) a cope. In Persia and Armenia they wear a cap with fur border called the *kulpas*. Married priests wear a blue cassock, a black gown, and a blue turban.

The vestments of the Nestorian Church are

perhaps the simplest of the forms of dress in vogue in the various non-reformed Churches. They are six in number, and are respectively called the *prazôna, peena, zunnâra, hurrâra, estla* or *shorshippa,* and *msâne.* These correspond respectively to breeches, surplice, or alb, girdle, stole, chasuble, and shoes, but they differ in some degree from the analogous vestments in use elsewhere. They are all made of white linen or calico, the only colour employed being in the girdle and stole, which (to use the convenient heraldic terms) are checky in squares white and blue, bearing crosses of the same colours counterchanged. The chasuble, too, has a Latin cross worked on the back. The latter is a clumsy vestment, being simply a square cloth, thrown over the shoulders and held in position with the finger and thumb. The stole does not reach below the waist, and is kept in its place under the girdle. It is remarkable that the vestments of the different orders of clergy differ only in the quality of the material, and not in elaboration or form ; and that they are, as a general rule, only worn during the celebration of the Holy Eucharist or the administration of Baptism. At other services the priests usually wear their ordinary costume, which differs only slightly from that of laymen.

The following list will show the parallelism existing between the vestments of the East and of the West; it is useful as showing that the differences between them consist entirely in matters of detail, and not in essentials:

[vakass] = amice.
στοιχάριον = alb.
ἐπιμανίκια = maniple.
ἐπιτραχήλιον } = stole.
ὡράριον
ζώνη = girdle.
φαινόλιον = chasuble.
ἐπιγονάτιον may be compared with appendages of subcingulum.
ὠμοφόριον = pall.
μάνδυας = cope, approximately.
χαμαλαύχη } = mitre „
ἐξωχαμαλαύχη
πατέρεσσα = pastoral staff.
ἐγκόλπιον = pectoral cross.
σάκκος = dalmatic

Thus, the ἐπιγονάτιον, μάνδυας, χαμαλαύχη and ἐξωχαμαλαύχη have no exact equivalent in the West; while, on the other hand, the amice is only represented in one provincial church, and the tunicle, dalmatic, gloves, ring, stockings and sandals, have no Eastern vestments to correspond with them. This is just what we might expect, for these vestments are all, comparatively speaking, of mediaeval invention or application, and the Eastern Church, as we said in other words at the commencement of this chapter, preserves many of the primitive rites and usages in a condition much less altered by time than does its Western sister.

CHAPTER VI.

THE VESTMENTS OF THE REFORMED CHURCHES.

ONE of the main differences between a church unreformed and a church reformed lies in this: that in the former the externals of public worship are magnified in importance even to the minutest detail, while in the latter the weight attached to such matters is diminished in a greater or less degree.

Considerable variety is apparent in the importance attached by different reformed churches to these matters, and, in consequence, considerable variety is apparent in the extent to which they are elaborated. Those churches which at the Reformation retained the episcopate, retained with it, in a more or less modified form, many of the old usages; while those churches which abolished the hierarchical and restored the democratic system of church government, for the most part abolished the customs of their pre-reformation predecessors.

The Vestments of the Reformed Churches. 193

Perhaps among no bodies of Christians are the externals of worship so little heeded as among the English dissenting sects ; these, being composed of seceders from a reformed church, may be said to have undergone a double reformation, which has had the effect of expunging the last traces of ritual from their services. In the consequent neglect of order, the wearing of robes of office has become entirely optional, not only with the different sects, but even with the individual ministers ; and where a gown is worn, as no definite shape of gown is prescribed, the choice of robe remains optional. Hence, these bodies need not concern us further, as the discussion of their vestments would be merely an uninteresting and monotonous account of the practice of isolated modern congregations.

The four churches whose usage must occupy our attention in the present chapter are the Lutheran churches of Germany and Scandinavia, the Episcopal churches of England and of Spain, and the Presbyterian churches, with especial reference to the church of Scotland.

§ I. THE LUTHERAN CHURCHES.

Of all reformations, the least thorough, as far as outward observance was concerned, was the reformation in which Martin Luther played the leading part. In Lübeck is the brass of the

Lutheran Bishop Tydeman, who died in 1561, representing him in full Eucharistic vestments, in no wise differing from the vestments of his non-reformed predecessors. At the present day the predominance of the Evangelical church in Germany (as distinguished from the Lutheran) has abolished vestments, with the exception of the Geneva gown and its attendants, among the Protestants; but in Sweden and Denmark, where the Protestant Episcopal is still the national church, the old vestments, with some modifications and omissions, are retained.

The Lutheran minister of the present day in Sweden and Denmark is described as wearing an ample cassock, or black gown, and a white frilled ruff, or collar, both in his outdoor life and at morning and evening prayer. At the Communion Service he assumes an alb, or, rather, surplice— a white, ungirded garment, open down the front— over which is placed a chasuble with a large cross on the back.

The Swedish Kyrko-Handbog recognises there vestments: the *chorkappa*, *messhake* and *messe-sjorta*—answering to the cope, chasuble, and surplice, respectively.

§ II. THE ANGLICAN CHURCH.

The history of vestments and their usage in England subsequent to the reformation is not

The Vestments of the Reformed Churches. 195

lacking in complexity, and is rendered harder to unravel by the heated discussions carried on, and the contradictory assertions brought forward, at the present day by the various parties within the English church. It is no part of our duty here to give an account of the different recensions of the liturgy published and approved in the years after the reformation ; we are here only concerned with the rubrical directions which they contain to regulate the use of vestments permitted in the English church.

The first English Prayer-Book, published in 1549, contained the following injunction :

> 'Upon the day and at the time appointed for the ministration of the Holy Communion, the Priest that shall execute the holy ministry shall put upon him the vesture appointed for that ministration, that is to say, a white alb plain with a vestment or cope. And where there be many Priests or Deacons there so many shall be ready to help the Priest in the ministrations as shall be requisite ; and shall have upon them likewise the vestures appointed for their ministry, that is to say, albes with tunicles.'

It is quite clear, even without the documentary evidence which is forthcoming, that this was merely intended as temporary, as, indeed, was the whole 1549 Prayer-Book. In a letter which Fagius and Bucer addressed to their Strassburg friends, describing their reception by Archbishop Cranmer, there is given a short account of the ceremonies then in use. In the course of this letter, they say, 'We hear that some concessions have been made both to a respect for antiquity and to the infirmity of the present age, such, for instance, as the vestments commonly used in the Sacrament of the Eucharist.'

An inspection of the rubric will show that it was ingeniously designed to please all parties. The word 'vestment,' of course, means the chasuble, *the* vestment *par excellence*, and therefore often spoken of in that apparently general way. The 'alb and vestment' being specified did not *necessarily* exclude all the other vestments which were worn *between* these two. Hence those clergy who preferred the old rites and ceremonies might read the rubric into permitting, or even enjoining, the maintenance of the old vestments,* while those who subscribed to the principles of the reforming party might set at defiance all old usages by wearing the cope while celebrating the Communion.

Another rubric relating to vestments appears in the first Prayer-Book. This is the first rubric printed after the order for the Communion, and runs thus:

'Upon Wednesdays and Fridays the English Litany shall be said or sung in all places . . . and though there be none to communicate with the Priest, yet these days (after the

---

* With one modification only. The albs are expressly ordered to be worn *plain*.

The Vestments of the Reformed Churches. 197

Litany ended) the Priest shall put upon him a plain albe or surplice, with a cope, and say all things at the altar (appointed to be said at the celebration of the Lord's Supper) until after the offertory. . . .'

Finally, in this Prayer-Book also occurs the following :

'In the saying or singing of Mattins and Evensong, baptizing and burying, the minister in parish churches and chapels annexed to the same shall use a surplice. And in all cathedral churches and colleges the archdeacons, deans, provosts, masters, prebendaries, and fellows, being graduates, may use in the quire, besides their surplices, such hood as appertaineth to their several degrees. And whensoever the bishop shall celebrate the Holy Communion in the church, or execute any other public ministration, he shall have upon him, beside his rochet, a surplice or albe, and a cope or vestment, and also his pastoral staff in his hand, or else borne or holden by his chaplain.'

The revised Prayer-Book of 1552 is much more stringent in its reformation of vestment-use. It condescends to mention vestments but once, in a prohibitory rubric, which reduces vestment-use in the English Church to an almost Presbyterian simplicity. This rubric is as follows :

'And here it is to be noted that the minister at the time of the communion, and at all other times in his ministration, shall use neither albe, vestment, nor cope : but being archbishop or bishop, he shall have and wear a rochet: and being a priest or deacon, he shall have and wear a surplice only.'

In the Prayer-Book of 1559 a rubric is to be found requiring the restoration of the vestments and ornaments of the first Prayer-Book, thereby setting aside the order of the second Prayer-Book. At the consecration of Archbishop Parker in 1559, we are told that at morning prayer the archbishop-elect wore his academical robes. After the sermon, the archbishop-elect and the four attendant bishops proceeded to the vestry, and returned prepared for the communion service, the archbishop in a linen surplice, the Bishop of Chichester in a silk cope, the Bishops of Hereford and Bedford in linen surplices, but the Bishop of Exeter (Miles Coverdale) in a woollen cassock only. Two chaplains of the archbishop, who assisted the Bishop of Chichester at the communion service, also wore silk copes.

After the communion service they again proceeded to the vestry and returned, the archbishop in 'episcopal alb,' surplice, chimere of black silk, and a collar of precious sable-fur round his neck; the Bishops of Chichester and Hereford in episcopalia, namely, surplice and chimere. Coverdale and the Bishop of Bedford wore cassocks only.

This passage shows us that the right of private judgment was exercised, even at such an important ceremony as the consecration of an archbishop, in 1559 as now. The Puritan principles of Coverdale were given full sway even when acting in co-operation with his less austere brethren.

The Vestments of the Reformed Churches. 199

It also introduces us to a new vestment, the *chimere*, which is one of the greatest puzzles to be found in the subject of vestments. Since the Reformation, it has continued ever since as a dress peculiar to bishops, but its origin and the exact date of its introduction are uncertain.

The *chimere* is a short coat, properly without sleeves ; but in England the tailors of the Stuart period transferred the sleeves of the *rochet* to the *chimere*. Hence the modern English bishops wear sleeveless rochets and sleeved chimeres—both solecisms. The English chimere is black, though from the reign of Edward VI to that of Elizabeth it was scarlet ; but the form current on the Continent, a large cape called the *mantelletum*, is scarlet, and the chimere worn by the Roman prelates in England is purple.

It is not unlikely, from the appearance of the vestment, that it is a modification of the cope or almuce—possibly a combination of the two vestments.

In 1560 Thos Sampson writes complaining to Peter Martyr that 'three of our lately-appointed bishops are to officiate at the table of the Lord, one as priest, another as deacon, and a third as subdeacon, before the image of the crucifix, or at least not far from it, with candles, and habited in the golden vestments of the papacy.' This seems to indicate that at Court (where this was to take place) the old vestments were kept up. From a letter of Miles Coverdale's written in 1566, we learn that the square cap, bands, and tippet were enjoined to be worn out of doors ('Zurich Letters,' vol. i, p. 63, vol. ii, p. 121; Parker Society).

In all the subsequent Prayer-Books, the 'Ornaments Rubric,' as it is called, is the source of our information with respect to the vestments required to be worn in the English Church. This famous rubric runs thus (as given in the Prayer-Book of 1662):

'And here it is to be noted, that such ornaments of the church and of the ministers thereof, at all times of their ministration, shall be retained and be in use, as were in this Church of England, by the authority of Parliament, in the second year of the reign of King Edward the Sixth.'

The indefiniteness observed in the Edwardian rubrics, to which this injunction refers, invests the 'Ornaments Rubric' with a certain vagueness; and this is responsible for the long and violent strife that has waged around it, and for the chaotic condition of modern Anglican order, both in vestments and other observances.

Recent attempts have been made on the part of individual clergymen to introduce certain details of the ritual of the Western Church into the services of the Church of England. All such innovations are, however, regarded as illegal,

The Vestments of the Reformed Churches. 201

and clergymen attempting to introduce them lay themselves open to prosecution. The rulings in the case known as the Folkestone ritual case (Elphinstone *v.* Purchas) is the standard of reference in such matters. Among many other details, the use of the following vestments was declared absolutely contrary to the Ecclesiastical Law of England : The biretta, chasuble, alb, and tunicle at the Holy Communion ; the cope at Holy Communion except on high feast days in cathedrals and collegiate churches. On other occasions a decent and comely surplice is to be used by every minister saying the public prayers or administering the sacrament or other rites of the Church.*

This tendency to elaboration and to revival of mediaeval practices is not, however, altogether of modern growth. In Wells Cathedral is the effigy of Bishop Creighton, who died in 1672, clad in cassock, amice, alb, and cope, the latter with a jewelled border. On his head is a cap with side-flaps, over which is a *mitra pretiosa*. More singular still, considering that the person commemorated was an ardent reformer, is the brass of Bishop Goodrick at Ely Cathedral, who died in 1554.

* For a complete analysis of the 'Ornaments Rubric ' with elaborate historical and legal disquisitions, reference should be made to the published report of the Folkestone case (Kegan Paul, 1878).

He is represented in full Eucharistic vestments of the pre-Reformation period. Both these apparent anomalies are probably to be accounted for by the Romanizing tendency of the reigning monarchs under whom both these persons lived.

The vestments of the clergy did not escape the lash of the satirists of Queen Elizabeth's reign. About 1565, for instance, a tract was published entitled 'A pleasant Dialogue between a Soldier of Berwick and an English chaplain: wherein are largely handled and laid open such reasons as are brought for maintenance of Popish Traditions in our English Church.' The soldier speaks thus to Bernard, the priest : 'But, Bernard, I pray thee, tell me of thine honesty what was the cause that thou hast been in so many changes of apparel this forenoon, now black, now white, now in silk and gold, and now at length in this swouping black gown, and this sarcenet flaunting tippet.' This describes Bernard as first in his ordinary cassock or clerical dress ; then in his surplice for morning prayer; then in the cope for communion ; and, lastly, in the preaching gown and tippet. The passage is interesting, as it brings the practice of wearing a black gown at the sermon, once universal in the English Church, but now fast dying out, back almost to the reformation.

One more English church vestment remains to be noticed—the scarf. This is a broad black band of silk, which is worn like a stole, passed round the back of the neck and allowed to depend on either side. It is worn by doctors of divinity and by the clerical authorities of collegiate and cathedral bodies. Its origin is *possibly* to be found in the stole, but it is more probably a modification of an article of University costume.

During the imposition of Episcopacy upon Scotland in the Stuart period the dress of the clergy was of a form designed by no less a person than his Sacred Majesty King James I himself. At that monarch's own request the Parliament of 1609 passed an Act authorizing him to do so, assigning in its preface the reasons for this step to be 'that it had been found by daily experience that the greatness of his Majesty's empire, the magnificence of his Court, the fame of his wisdom, the civility of his subjects, were alluring princes and strangers from every part of the world, and that it was fitting that bishops and ministers, judges and magistrates, should appear before those in becoming apparel ; it was therefore referred to his Majesty's serene wisdom to devise appropriate garments and robes of office for these different functionaries.'

The result of this was an order 'that ministers should wear black clothes and in the pulpit black gowns ; that bishops and doctors of divinity should wear " black cassikins syde to their knee " [equivalent to the " bishop's apron " of the modern English prelate and the short Presbyterian cassock], black gowns above, and a black craip [scarf] about their necks. The bishops were ordained to have their gowns with *lumbard* sleeves, according to the form of England, with tippets and craips about their craigs [necks].'

In 1631 Charles I directed the *surplice* to be worn. In 1633, when he visited Scotland, the bishops and chaplains officiated before him in surplices. He induced Parliament to pass an Act like that of 1609, giving him the power to regulate clerical costume; but this was so much objected to by the clergy themselves (some of whom expressed a fear that his Majesty would order them to wear 'hoods and bells'), that in 1634 they petitioned the King not to interfere with the arrangements of his predecessor; and their request seems to have been granted.

§ III. The Reformed Churches of Spain and Portugal.

The practices of both these churches are commendably simple: a white tunic, or surplice, and a white stole, are the only vestments or ornaments at any time to be worn, except in sermons or at funerals, when a black gown *may* be assumed. Deacons wear their stoles in the ancient diaconal

The Vestments of the Reformed Churches. 205

fashion, *i.e.*, over the left shoulder and under the right arm ; presbyters wear theirs round the neck and hanging straight down.

§ IV. THE PRESBYTERIAN CHURCH.

We have already shown that in Apostolic times, and the first few years of the post-Apostolic

FIG. 29.—A SYNOD MEETING OF THE REFORMED CHURCH OF FRANCE.

period, robes of office were not worn by the officiating minister. Vestments do not meet us until the moderatorship of the Ecclesiastical Assemblies had crystallized into the Episcopate.

The oldest Christian organization now existing

in which the diordinal system of government has been restored is undoubtedly the Waldensian church. Although this church has not been *proved* to be older than the thirteenth century, it cannot be asserted that its foundation is not anterior to that date ; an impenetrable mist— rendered more obscure, it must be admitted, by the doubtful authenticity of many of the church documents—shrouds its early years. Unfortunately it cannot be discovered whether its clergy wore any distinctive robes when conducting its services. The chroniclers have not thought it worth their while to tell us, but it is improbable that anything very elaborate was worn, as a church which made a change so drastic as the abolition of the Episcopate would be unlikely to maintain the elaborate accessories of the non-reformed church. At present the simple black gown is worn, as in all other branches of the Presbyterian church throughout the world.

The task of compiling details regarding the vestments of the Presbyterian church is rendered easy by the small account which that church, in all its sections, takes of ritual matters ; but the same cause also increases its difficulty in another direction. Paradoxical as this statement may appear, it becomes intelligible when we reflect that but few Presbyterian assemblies would consider it consistent with their dignity to take any notice of

The Vestments of the Reformed Churches.

matters of dress, personal or official ; while on the other hand few Presbyterian writers have thought such matters worthy of their notice. The writer has referred to liturgies in the English, French, German, Roumanian, and other languages, representing the chief reformed Churches of Europe holding the Presbyterian system, but has failed to find any rubrical direction or reference containing any information. The collecting of material is thus simplified by the small amount of material actually available, but rendered difficult by the baldness of the records in which the materials have to be sought.

The vestments worn by clergy of the Presbyterian Churches are not so much ecclesiastical as professional or academical, like the barrister's gown. They are at most four in number : the cassock, scarf, bands, and gown, to which the hood of the wearer's degree is added.

The cassock is a somewhat ugly garment of black silk, which resembles an ordinary short coat ; it rarely reaches as far as the knees. There can be no doubt that it is a modification, for convenience' sake, of the long cassock worn by clergy of the Episcopal Churches, which was the inner garment, university and clerical, of the middle ages. The scarf is a long strip of black cloth, wound sash-wise round the waist and knotted in front. The bands are two short pendant tails of white lawn, hanging in front, now fastened round the neck by an elastic cord. These survive in the universities as well as in the Presbyterian Church. The name was originally applied to the Elizabethan ruff, in which must be sought the prototype of the ecclesiastical bands ; and the use of a cylindrical box to keep the ruff in has caused the survival of the old meaning of the word in 'bandbox.' The stiff starched or propped band passed at the commencement of the seventeenth century into the *falling band* (not unlike a modern child's lace collar), of which the ecclesiastical 'bands' is the diminution.

The gown is of the pattern known as the Geneva gown—a black silk gown with ample sleeves and faced with velvet.

It should be here remarked that there is considerable laxity in individual usage. The cassock and scarf are almost universally discarded, and, in fact, they were probably never very generally worn. For the Geneva gown is often substituted the gown proper to the university degree of the wearer.

Very few regulations affecting robes have been passed by any of the assemblies of the churches in the Presbyterian Alliance. The General Assembly of the Church of Scotland in 1575 passed an important injunction, which, however, refers rather to personal than to official attire. As it is a curious document, we give it here in full :

The Vestments of the Reformed Churches. 209

'For as muche as a comelie and decent apparrell is requisite in all, namelie, ministers, and suche as beare functioun in the kirk, first, we thinke all kinde of browdering [broidering] unseemlie; all begaires [coloured stripes] of velvet, in gowne, hose, or coat, and all superfluous and vaine cutting out, steeking [stitching] with silkes, all kinde of costlie sewing on pasments [laces], or sumptuous and large steeking with silkes; all kinde of costlie sewing or variant hewes in sarkes; all kinde of light and variant hewes in clothing, as reid, blew, yellow, and suche like, which declare the lightnesse of the minde; all wearing of rings, bracelets, buttons of silver, gold, or other mettall; all kinds of superfluiteis of cloath in making of hose; all using of plaids in the kirk by readers or ministers, namelie, in the time of their ministrie and using their office; all kinde of gownning, cutting, doubletting, or breekes of velvet, satine, taffatie or suche like; and costlie giltings of whingers and knives, and suche like; all silk hatts, and hatts of diverse and light colours; but that their whole habite be of grave colour, as blacke, russett, sad gray, sad browne; or searges, worsett, chamlett, grogram, lylis, worset, or suche like; that the good Word of God, by them and their immoderatenesse, be not slandered.'*

There is one rule, or rather unwritten convention, affecting the wearing of vestments in the Presbyterian Church, at least, in the British Islands. The *bands* are regarded as an indication that their wearer is the minister of a recognised congregation; hence, when an ordained minister of the Presbyterian Church who does not hold such an

* Calderwood, 'Historie of the Kirk of Scotland' (Wodrow Society), vol. iii, p. 354.

office happens to be conducting a service, he does not wear bands.

The Geneva gown has not always been worn in the Presbyterian Churches abroad. Thus in the Church of Holland, till recently, the official costume of a minister was a picturesque uniform, consisting of the old three-cornered hat, and a coat resembling the ordinary evening-dress coat, having a long pleated strip called the 'mantle' hooked on the neck, obviously a survival from an earlier and more ample gown of some kind, knee-breeches, buckled at the knees, and buckled shoes. This costume was worn only when the minister was officiating at service. It has now, however, been universally abandoned for the Geneva gown.

The gown and bands, with or without the cassock and scarf, are now worn only at Divine Service; but in the early part of the seventeenth century (in Britain as on the Continent) they were worn by ministers sitting in assembly as well, in accordance with the decree of the Synod of Fife, which in 1611 ordained that ministers should attend meetings in the exercise of Synodal assembly in black gowns and other abulʒiements* prescribed in the Act of Parliament.

The elders never wear any insignia of office, and never have done so.

* Habiliments.

CHAPTER VII.

THE RITUAL USES OF VESTMENTS.

WE have now described the form and ornamentation of the different vestments worn by the clergy of the principal sections of Christendom ; but we have only incidentally touched upon another and equally important matter, namely, when and how these vestments were worn, and the liturgical practices connected with them. A more extended account of these matters will be the subject of the present chapter.

The non-reformed Western and Eastern Churches alone need occupy our attention. The vestment uses of the various reformed churches are practically *nil*, and all available details concerning these Churches have already been given in the preceding chapter.

Vestments were obtained by a church or a cathedral in many ways. They were often embroidered for presentation to the church by ladies, who found in the work of embroidery an easy and pleasant way of passing the time ; or else by the inmates of nunneries as a religious work. Some were presented as expiatory offerings by conscience-stricken laymen ; others bequeathed as a perpetual memorial by incumbents or prelates. Others, again, were purchased with money mulcted as compensation for sins.

The first sacred function in which any vestment took part was its own benediction. This was always spoken by a bishop, and was in form of prayers said over all the vestments of a suit together, and the individual vestments separately. The following may be taken as specimens of these dedicatory prayers ; it is unnecessary to occupy space in giving all, as complete sets can be found in any Pontifical:

Benedictio omnium vestimentorum simul.—Omnipotens Deus qui per Moisen famulum tuum pontificalia et sacerdotalia ac levitica vestimenta ad explendum ministerium eorum in conspectu tuo, et ad decorem tui nominis, per nostre humilitatis servitutem pontificare ✠ benedicere ✠ consecrare digneris ✠ ut divinis cultibus et sacris misteriis apta et benedicta existant ; hiisque sacris vestibus pontifices, sacerdotes seu levite tui induti ab omnibus impulsionibus seu temptacionibus malignorum spirituum muniti et defensi esse mereantur, tuisque ministeriis apte et condigne servire et inherere, atque in hiis placide tibi et devote perseverare tribue. Per Christum. Oremus.

Deus invicte virtutis auctor, et omnium rerum creator ac sanctificator, intende propicius ad preces nostras, et hec indumenta levitice et sacerdotalis glorie ministris tuis sumenda tuo ore proprio benedicere ✠ sanctificare ✠ et consecrare digneris omnesque eis utentes, tuis misteriis aptos, et tibi in eis devote et amicabiliter servientes gratos effici concedas. Per Christum Dominum.

Benedictio Amicti.—Oremus. Benedic Domine quesume omnipotens Deus amictum istum levitici seu sacerdotalis officii et concede propicius ut quicumque eum capiti suo imposuerit benedictionem tuam accipiat; sitque in fide solidus et sanctitatis gravedine fundatus. Per Christum. Etc.

The vestment thus dedicated was sprinkled with holy water after each prayer.

The ritual uses of vestments may be conveniently described in two parts; discussing in the first the persons by whom they were worn, and, in the second, the occasions upon which, and the manner in which, they were worn.

The vestments were distributed among the different orders of clergy in a manner similar to that in which the early vestments of the second period were allotted (see p. 28), but on a more complex system, as befitted their greater elaboration. Some hints of this system have already been given in the preceding pages; it will be convenient here to amplify this information.

The seven orders of the Western Church are the three minor orders (*ostiarius, lector, acolytus*), and the four major orders (subdeacons, deacons, priests, and bishops; we may divide the last into three subdivisions, bishops proper, archbishops, and the Pope). All ranks wore the *alb*, and all the major orders the *maniple*. All those above the rank of subdeacon wore *amice* and *stole*, and all above the rank of deacon the *chasuble*. Subdeacons were distinguished by the *tunicle*, deacons by the *dalmatic*; both vestments were added to the outfit of bishops, the latter with a remarkable distinction already described (p. 79). The *stockings, sandals, subcingulum* (originally), *mitre, gloves, ring*, and *staff* were peculiar to bishops and to certain abbots to whom these *pontificalia* had been expressly granted by the Pope.* Archbishops added the *pall* to this lengthy catalogue, and the Pope (who dispensed with the pastoral staff) reserved the *orale*, and in later times the *subcingulum*, for his exclusive use.

We now turn to the consideration of the occasions upon which, and the manner in which, these vestments were worn.

The vestments worn at the mass by the celebrant and his assistants were those which we have described under the heading of 'Eucharistic Vestments,' and of these one, the chasuble, was worn exclusively at this service and at no other.

In Advent, and between Septuagesima and Easter, the deacons and subdeacons were directed

* When the abbot of a monastery was also a bishop, the *prior* had also the right to wear *pontificalia* when his superior was absent.

to substitute chasubles for their dalmatics or tunicles; and these chasubles were ordered to be worn, not in the usual manner, but folded, and passed across the breast like the diaconal stole. That is to say, the chasuble, which must have been of a flexible* material, was folded into a strip as narrow as possible, and secured over the shoulder and under the girdle of the alb. These were not to be worn during the whole service, however; the subdeacon had to remove his folded chasuble at the Epistle; at the Gospel the deacon had to cross his over the left arm, and so keep it till after the post-communion.

There is but one representation of a deacon so vested known to exist in England. It is one of a series of sculptured effigies of ecclesiastics on the north-west tower of Wells Cathedral. These have been described by Mr St John Hope in 'Archæologia,' vol. liv. We give here the figure to which special reference is at present being made. Besides the chasuble, the effigy is vested in cassock, amice, alb, and girdle; and a book, probably meant for the Gospels, is represented as carried in the hand.

It should be observed that at the mass of a

* The difficulty of folding the chasuble without injuring it has led to the substitution of a broad purple stole-like vestment, worn exactly like the folded chasuble. This is called the *stolone*.

216   *Ecclesiastical Vestments.*

feast falling within the limits of time prescribed, the ordinary dalmatic and tunicle were worn in the ordinary way.

FIG. 30.—DEACON IN FOLDED CHASUBLE, WELLS CATHEDRAL.

This peculiar custom was unknown to the Franciscans. The deacons of this order put off

The Ritual Uses of Vestments. 217

the dalmatic entirely upon fast-days, and did not substitute any other vestment for it; a similar practice, with respect to the tunicle, was observed by the subdeacons, so that the deacons wore *alb* and *stole* only, the subdeacons *alb* and *maniple*. This practice was not observed at the Vigils of Saints, or of the Nativity, and on a few other occasions.

When a cleric of sacerdotal rank *ministered* (as opposed to *celebrated*) at the mass, his dress was the amice, the alb, the stole, and the *cope*. The same vestments are worn by the priest at the mass of the pre-sanctified* on Good Friday.

Before the vestments are put on for the mass the priest must wash his hands, and prepare the chalice, placing over it the purificator or napkin used for wiping the sacred vessels. Above the purificator he places the paten, with an unbroken host, and covers it with a small linen cloth, over which he puts the burse. This done, he takes the vestments one by one; he first receives the amice, takes it by its ends and strings, and kisses the middle of it where there is a cross. A prelate, it should be noticed, always puts on a surplice before vesting. The amice being put in its place, the alb and girdle are then assumed, then the maniple and chasuble. Each vestment is kissed

* The Sacrament when used on a day when the Eucharist service is not gone through in its entirety.

before being put on, and a prayer said with the assumption of each; these prayers differ little in style from those said in the similar ceremony in the Eastern Church, and it has therefore been thought unnecessary to give them here.

In an inventory of the Vestry of Westminster Abbey,* the following directions are given in a late fifteenth-century hand :

The Revestyng of the abbot of Westm' att evensong.—ffyrst the westerer shall lay the abbots cope lowest opon the awter w^t in the sayd westre, nex opon hys gray Ames, then hys surples, after that hys Rochett and uppermost his Kerchure.

Hys Myter & crose beyng Redy w^t hys glovys and pontyfycalls.

The Revestyng of the sayd abbot att syngyng by Masse.— Fyrst the westerer shall lay lowest the chesebell, a bove that the dalmatyke and the dalmatyk w^t ye longest slevys uppermost, & the other nethermost then hys stole & hys fanane and hys gyrdyll, opon that his albe theropon his gray Ames a bove that hys Rochett and uppermost hys kerchur w^t a vestry gyrdyll to tukk up his cole.

Hys Miter & crose beyng Redy w^t hys glovys and pontyfycalls And a fore all thys you muste se that hys sabatyns & syndalls be Redy at hys first cūyng whan he settyth hym downe in the travys.

This direction is important in one respect. It shows us the order in which the vestments were put on, it is true; that, however, one would naturally infer from the order in which they are

* Edited by Dr Wickham Legg in 'Archaeologia,' vol. lii., p. 195.

seen in the monuments. But it tells us also that a canon wore his canonical habit underneath his mass habit at high mass, but so arranged that it should be, as far as possible, out of sight; hence the direction to have ' a vestry girdle to tuck up his cowl.' At Wells, Hereford, and Norwich Cathedrals are to be seen figures of canons, the almuce or amess appearing at the neck, although they are vested in eucharistic habit.

The duty of the minister, as far as the vestments of the celebrant are concerned, consists in seeing that the vestments are laid out in their proper order on a table in the vestry, or, should there be no vestry, on a side-table near the altar (never on the altar itself); the vestments for the assistant should be on the right-hand side of those for the celebrant, the vestments for the deacon and subdeacon on the left. He should also see that each is properly put on, especially that the alb is drawn through the girdle so as to overhang it and to be raised about a finger's breadth from the ground, and that the chasuble is straight. He must especially be careful that the assistant does not put on his cope before the priest puts on his chasuble. During the celebration he has to see that the chasuble is not disarranged by genuflexions, and to raise the chasuble so as to give complete freedom to the priest's arms at the elevation of the host. After the celebration the vestments are taken off with similar ceremonies in the reverse order.

On Ember days, Rogations, in processions, and when the Sunday or Saint's day mass is said in the chapter house, on Ash Wednesday, Good Friday, and Palm Sunday, albs and amices only are to be worn by the ministers.

The dress at the ordinary offices (mattins, lauds, etc.) is amice, alb, stole, and cope; a brass at Horsham represents a priest so vested, and has the merit of showing the exact manner in which the stole should be crossed. This combination of vestments was also worn at benedictions, at absolution after a mass for the dead, and, as just remarked, by the assistant at mass if a priest, and by the celebrant at the mass of the pre-sanctified. 'The cope,' the rubric tells us, 'is not strictly a sacerdotal vestment, but it is worn by the rulers of the choir and others.'

The clergy in choir wear black (choral) copes, except on principal doubles,* and on the doubles falling on Sunday, when silk copes of the colour of the day are worn. On the vigil of Easter, and

* Feasts were divided into Doubles, Simples, and Sundays. Doubles were so-called from the anthems being *doubled, i.e.,* said throughout at the beginning and end of the Psalms in the breviary office, instead of the first words only being said. The principal doubles were Christmas, Epiphany, Easter, Ascension, Whitsunday, Assumption, the Local Anniversary, and the Dedication of the Church.

through and on the octave, they wore surplices only, as also on doubles occurring from Easter to Michaelmas.

If a bishop celebrate, and if it be Maunday Thursday, or Whitsunday, he has seven deacons, seven subdeacons, and three acolytes—on other doubles only five. On feasts with Rulers, two at least; on Good Friday only one. The rulers of the choir were those whose duty it was to chant the office and Kyrie at mass, and to superintend the choristers. On doubles these were four in number, on simples two. Rulers wore silk copes of the colour of the day over a surplice, and had silver staves as emblems of office.

The Roman Pontifical lays down succinct rules for the vesting of a bishop for the different duties of his position. These are as follows :

Confirmation.—White cope and stole, amice, rochet, mitra aurifrigiata.

Ordinations.—As for high mass : colour according to the day.

Consecration of a Bishop.—The consecrator as for high mass : colour according to the day; each of the two assistant-bishops in rochet, cope, amice, stole, and mitra simplex.

Profession of a Nun.—As for high mass.

Coronation of a Sovereign. — As for high mass : colour according to day; each of the assistant-bishops in rochet, amice, white stole and cope, mitra simplex. In England all the bishops used to wear full pontificalia.

Laying the Foundation of a Church.—Rochet, amice, white stole and cope, mitra simplex, pastoral staff.

Consecration of a Church.—The same till the mass, then full pontificalia (white).
Reconciliation of a Church.—The same.
Consecration of the Holy Oil on Maunday Thursday.—Full (white) pontificalia, mitra pretiosa.
At a Synod held in a Cathedral Church.—Rochet, amice, red stole, red cope, mitra pretiosa.
Procession of Palms.—Alb, amice, purple stole, purple cope, mitra simplex.
Procession of Corpus Christi.—Alb, amice, stole, tunic, dalmatic, white cope; a mitra pretiosa borne behind. In England and in France red was the colour.
Rogation Days. — Alb, amice, purple stole, purple cope, mitra simplex.

In occasional services, such as baptism, a surplice and stole are worn. At baptisms two stoles are used, one of violet, which is worn at the first part of the service, and the other of white, which is substituted for the first in the course of the office. This observance has a symbolical meaning; violet being the colour which typifies sin and penitence, and white being associated with ideas of purity, the change in the stole is emblematic of the regenerating change which the rite of baptism is supposed to work. A reversible stole, violet on one side and white on the other, is sometimes used for this service. In processions and benedictions at the altar (*i.e.*, blessings of wax, images, etc.) the cope must be worn. In other benedictions stole and surplice are sufficient.

The Ritual Uses of Vestments. 223

The cope must also be worn at an absolution after a mass for the dead ; the colour of the cope for such a service is black, the ministers lay aside their dalmatics, and when the celebrant assumes the cope he must lay aside his maniple. If for any reason a cope be not obtainable, these rites (benedictions, absolutions, etc.) must be performed in alb and crossed stole only, without chasuble or maniple.

Should it be found necessary to celebrate high mass without the aid of a deacon or subdeacon, the Epistle is ordered to be sung by a lector vested in a surplice.

We must now approach an important branch of this complex subject—the varieties in the colour of the vestments depending on the character of the day, in other words, the liturgical colours of the vestments.

It does not appear that the definite assigning of particular colours to particular days is of older date than Innocent III's time; but before him, and even as far back as the time of the fathers of the church, we find that the early Christians had symbolical associations with colours, which have formed the foundation on which the elaborate structure of later times was built.

It is a matter of common knowledge that there are associations of sentiment and colour which are practically indissoluble. Black and sorrowful, white (or bright) and joyful, are synonymous terms, and similar expressions are universal.

White, in the first ten centuries of Christianity, typified purity and truth. Saints, angels, and Our Lord are for that reason represented clothed in white. As we have seen, the earliest vestments were probably white; the newly-baptized wore white during the week after baptism, and the dead were shrouded in white; the latter, however, probably more for convenience than for any symbolic reason.

Red, the colour of flame, was associated with ideas of warm, burning love. Our Lord is sometimes represented in red when performing works of mercy.

Green, the colour of plants, was regarded as typifying life, and sacred or beatified persons are sometimes depicted as clothed in this colour in reference to their everlasting life. Lastly,

Violet, which is formed by a mixture of red and black, was said to symbolize 'the union of love and pain in repentance.' It also typifies sorrow, without any reference to sin as its cause; thus the *Mater Dolorosa* is occasionally represented in a violet robe.*

Further than this we cannot go, and perhaps we have said too much. It is quite possible that these

* These explanations of colours are taken from Smith and Cheetham's 'Dictionary of Christian Antiquities.'

theories may have been put forward to account for phenomena which depended entirely on the taste and whim of the painters. It is well known that in the early ages of Christianity ideas of colour were vague, and yellow and green, dark blue and black, light blue and violet, were all regarded as being the same colour. Previous to the tenth century, it is quite true that coloured vestments are to be seen in mosaics and fresco-paintings; but the combinations of colours are such as to leave no doubt that they were simply adopted by the painter as convenient aids to distinguishing the various vestments from the surrounding background and from each other.

Coming now to Innocent III, we find that he prescribes four liturgical colours, white, red, black and green. These were the principal or primary liturgical colours; but there are others, secondary to these, which were modifications in tint of the primaries. Thus, properly, red is the colour of *martyrs*, white the colour of virgins; but there is a secondary colour, saffron, for *confessors*, and the secondaries, rose and lily, are considered interchangeable with red and white.

Hopelessly at variance are the practices throughout the Western Church, and we will not attempt to give more than a brief outline of the general principles. For those who desire fuller information reference is made to a paper by Dr Wickham

Legg in the first volume of the Transactions of the St Paul's Ecclesiological Society, in which no less than sixty-three different 'uses' are analyzed and tabulated, or compared.

The rules to which we have just referred are almost the only regulations respecting which uniform use prevails. For obvious reasons, white is appropriated to feasts of St Mary and of the other virgin saints; black is appropriated to the office of the dead; and red to the feasts of martyrs. Usually white is used for Christmas and Easter, and red for Whitsuntide and Feasts of Apostles. As a general rule, however, the same sentimental associations are to be seen with colours in the middle ages as may possibly be traced in earlier times: *violet* being essentially penitential in its character, *red* being indicative of fire, blood or love, *white* of purity and joy, *black* of mourning, and *green* of life. Hence *violet* is the usual colour for Advent and Lent, *red* for feasts of martyrs, apostles and evangelists, and in some uses for Passion-tide and Easter; *white* for Christmas, feasts of virgins, Easter, and sometimes Michaelmas and All Saints; *black* for Good Friday and offices of the dead; *green* from the Octave of Epiphany to Candlemas, and from Trinity to Advent. The use of the last colour is, however, very arbitrary; it only occurs at one or two seasons in the year in each diocese, and these are very diverse.

The following is the Roman sequence of colours for the year, and it may be taken as an example of all:

> Advent to Christmas Eve : black or violet.
> Christmas Eve, if a Sunday : rose.
> Christmas Day : white.
> St Stephen : red.
> St John the Evangelist : white.
> Holy Innocents : violet ; red if a Sunday.
> Circumcision : white.
> Epiphany : white.
> Candlemas : violet for the procession of candles before mass, then white.
> Septuagesima to Maunday Thursday : violet.
> Good Friday : black.
> Easter : white.
> Ascension : white.
> Rogation Days : violet.
> Pentecost : red.
> Trinity Sunday : white.
> Corpus Christi : white.
> Trinity to Advent : green.
> Feasts of the Virgin Mary : white.
> St John Baptist : white.
> St Michael : white.
> All Saints : white.
> Martyrs : red.
> Apostles : red.
> Evangelists : red.
> Confessors : white.

Virgins: white.
Transfiguration: white.
Holy Cross: red.
Confirmation: white.
Dedication of a Church: white.
Harvest Festivals: white.
Requiem: black.

One or two miscellaneous points may be worth a passing notice before we bring our account of the vestments of the Western Church to a close.

During Lent it was the practice to cover up the images in the church with a curtain called the *velum quadrigesimale*. In the Fabric Rolls of York, for instance, we read the following entry (Anno 1518, 1519):

'Pro coloribus ad pingendum caminos de novo factos et pro c fauthoms cordarum pro suspensione pannorum quadrigesimalium ante novum crucifixum ivs.

'Pro pictione unius panni pendentis coram novo crucifixo in tempore quadrigesimali, et pro les curtayn ringes et pro les laic ac pro suicione alterius panni xiis.'

A point respecting the *ring* is worth mention. Doctors of Divinity and bishops only may wear a ring in the Western Church, and the former must take it off when celebrating mass.

Besides the Episcopal and Diaconal *dalmatic*, there is a third kind, to which allusion must be made: the Imperial dalmatic, which from time immemorial has been placed on the sovereigns of Europe at their coronation.

The Imperial Dalmatic in the treasury of St Peter's at Rome is thus described:

'It is laid upon a foundation of deep blue silk, having four different subjects on the shoulders behind and in front, exhibiting—although taken from different actions—the glorification of the body of our Lord. The whole has been carefully wrought with gold tambour and silk, and the numerous figures (as many as fifty-four) surrounding our Redeemer, who sits enthroned on a rainbow in the centre, display simplicity and gracefulness of design. The field of the vestment is powdered with flowers and crosses of gold and silver, having the bottom enriched with a running floriated pattern. It has also a representation of paradise, wherein the flowers, carried by tigers of gold, are of emerald green, turquoise blue, and flame colour. Crosses of silver cantonned with tears of gold, and of gold cantonned with tears of silver alternately, are inserted in the flowing foliage at the edge. Other crosses within circles are also placed after the same rule, when of gold in medallions of silver, and when of silver in the reverse order.

'This vestment is assigned to the 12th century. It has been conjectured that this dalmatic was formerly used by the German emperors when they were consecrated and crowned, and when they assisted the pope at the office of mass. On such occasions the emperor discharged the functions of subdeacon or deacon, and, clothed with a dalmatic, chanted the Epistle and Gospel ; in illustration of this custom it may be remarked that several of the German Emperors took part in the service, even so late as Charles V, who sung the Gospel at Boulogne in 1529. The dalmatic was, in fact, in those times, as it continues at the present day, both a regal and ecclesiastical habit, and it has constantly been the custom of European kingdoms for the sovereigns to wear it at their coronation.'*

* Rev. C. H. Hartshorne in *Arch. Journal.*

But the Ecclesiastical nature of the regal costume of the middle ages does not end with the dalmatic. Thus, the effigy of Richard I. at Fontevraud wears a cope-like mantle, a dalmatic, and a white sub-tunic, answering to the distinctive costumes of bishop or priest, deacon and sub-deacon respectively. When the body of Edward I was exhumed at Westminster in 1774, he was found to wear among other garments a dalmatic and a *stole*, crossed on the breast in the priestly manner. The body of John, in Worcester, was found in 1797 to be habited in costume similar to that represented on his effigy, with the addition of a monk's cowl, no doubt adopted in order to safeguard his prospects of future happiness, as death in the monastic habit was regarded as ensuring a passport to heaven.

The vestments of the Eastern Church are much simpler, and the rites connected with them have nothing like the complexity associated with those of the Western Church. They have but two colours, for instance—violet for fast-days (including Lent),* and white for the rest of the year—and ridicule the elaboration to which liturgical colours have been brought in the Western Church. This fact might be indicated, if any disproof of the existence of a primitive system of liturgical colours were needed.

* Violet or purple στοιχάρια are worn throughout Lent, except on Annunciation Day, Palm Sunday, and Easter Eve.

The Ritual Uses of Vestments. 231

The following are the rubrical directions and prayers used at vesting for the Eucharistic service in the Greek Church:

Being then come within the altar [after the procession up the church] they [the priest and deacon] make three bows before the holy table, and kiss the holy gospel and the holy table: then each, taking his στοιχάριον in his hand, makes three bows and saith softly to himself:

O God, purify me, a sinner, and have mercy upon me.

The Deacon comes to the priest, holds his στοιχάριον and ὡράριον in his right hand, and bowing down his head to him, saith:

Bless, sir, the στοιχάριον and the ὡράριον.

The priest. Blessed be our God always, now and for ever, even unto ages of ages.

The deacon then goes apart on one side of the altar ana puts on his στοιχάριον, saying:

My soul shall rejoice in the Lord, for He hath put on me the robe of salvation, and clothed me with the garment of gladness: as a bridegroom hath He put a crown on my head and decked me like a bride.

Then, kissing the ὡράριον, he puts it upon his left shoulder. Then he puts on his ἐπιμανίκια: putting on that on his right hand, he saith:

Thy right hand, O Lord, is glorified in strength; Thy right hand, O Lord, hath destroyed the enemies, and in the greatness of Thy glory hast Thou put down the adversaries.

Then, putting the other on his left hand:

Thy hands have made me and fashioned me. O give me understanding that I may learn Thy commandments.

[*He then prepares the sacred vessels.*]

The priest puts on his sacred vestments in the following manner. First, taking up his στοιχάριον in his left hand, and making three bows towards the east, he signs it with the sign of the cross, saying:

Ecclesiastical Vestments.

Blessed be our God always, etc.

And then he puts it on, saying, My soul shall rejoice, etc., *as the deacon said above.*

Next he takes up the επιτραχήλιον, *and, blessing it, he saith:*

Blessed be God who poureth out His grace on His priests, like the precious ointment upon the head that ran down unto the beard, even unto Aaron's beard, and went down to the skirts of his clothing.

He then takes the ζώνη, *and girding himself therewith, saith:*

Blessed be God who hath girded me with strength, and hath put me in the right way, making my feet like harts' feet, and hath set me up on high.

He next puts on his επιμανίκια, *saying as was said above by the deacon. After which he takes up his* επιγονάτιον, *if he be of such dignity as to wear one, and blessing it and kissing it, saith:*

Gird thee with thy sword upon thy thigh, O thou most mighty, according to thy worship and renown. Good luck have thou with thine honour, ride on because of the word of truth, of meekness, and righteousness, and thy right hand shall teach thee terrible things : always, now and for ever, even unto ages of ages. Amen.

Then he takes his φελώνιον, *and blesses and kisses it, saying:*

Let thy priests, O Lord, be clothed with righteousness, and let thy saints sing with joyfulness : always, now and for ever, even unto ages of ages. Amen.*

When the vestments are put off after the communion, the priest says *Nunc Dimittis*, τρισάγιον, and *Pater Noster*.

It does not appear that any complex rules hold good in the Greek Church respecting the vestments to be worn on certain days in the Church's year.

* Translation from King's 'Rites and Ceremonies of the Greek Church in Russia.'

The following synopsis of the vestment uses in the ordination service will show most clearly the nature and distribution of Ecclesiastical vestments in the Eastern Church.

Ordination of a Reader: A short φαινόλιον put on by the bishop, which is presently removed by the sub-deacons; the στοιχάριον is then blessed and put on by the bishop.

Ordination of a Sub-deacon: The candidate comes dressed in the στοιχάριον; the subdeacons hand the ὡράριον to the bishop, who signs it on the cross; the new sub-deacon kisses the cross and the bishop's hand, and girds himself with the ὡράριον.

Ordination of a Deacon: The candidate kneels before the altar; the bishop, at the beginning of the service, puts the end of the ὠμοφόριον upon him. After the service the bishop takes the ὡράριον and puts it on the new deacon's left shoulder, saying ἄξιος, which is repeated thrice by the choir; then the bishop gives him the ἐπιμανίκια, and ἄξιος is repeated as before. The fan (for blowing flies from the table) is presented after this, with the same words.

Ordination of a Priest: At the commencement the candidate kneels at the altar, and the bishop puts the ὠμοφόριον on his head. At the end the ὡράριον is taken from him, and the ἐπιτραχήλιον is received by the bishop, who kisses it; the newly-ordained priest kisses the vestment and the bishop's hand; the bishop puts it on the priest, saying ἄξιος, which is repeated as at the ordination of a deacon. The ζώνη and φαινόλιον is then conferred in a similar manner.

Ordination of a Bishop: The new bishop comes to the service in all his sacred vestments. At the end the ὠμοφόριον is put upon the elect, except when the consecration takes place in the see of the bishop, in which case the σάκκος and the other episcopal garments are given first. The same ceremonial is repeated as at the other ordinations.

The vestments worn at the administration of baptism are the φαινόλιον and επιμανίκια.

There are three orders of devotees in the Greek monasteries. The *probationers* wear a black cassock or vest called *shaesa*, and a hood (Russian *kamelauch*, χαμαλαύχη). The *proficients* wear, in addition, an upper cloak (μάνδυας). The *perfect* are distinguished by their hood or vail, which perpetually conceals their faces from sight.

APPENDIX I.

COSTUMES OF THE RELIGIOUS ORDERS.

THE following appendix does not profess to furnish more than an outline of the extensive subject with which it deals; for further details, as well as for illustrations of members of each of the orders, reference must be made to the great work of Bonanni, cited in Appendix III. Bonanni names the different habits rather loosely; in the main his nomenclature has been followed, but brought to a more uniform system.

Monks.

The dress of monks usually consists of the *vestis*, tunic or closed gown; the *scapular*, roughly speaking, a narrow, chasuble-like dress, with the front and back portions rectangular and of uniform width throughout; one or more open gowns (*pallium* or *cappa*); and the *caputium* or hood, fastened at the back and capable of being drawn over the head. 'Discalced' is not always to be taken in its fullest significance, or as signifying more than simply 'sandaled.' Different vestments are worn by individual orders or houses; the nature of these will be self-evident from their names.

1. ALEXIANS.—Black vestis and pallium, both reaching a little below the knee: caputium.

2. AMBROSE, ST.—Dark-coloured gown with cappa and scapular. Discalced.

3. ANTONIUS, ST (*Armenia*).—Ample black tunic, girded, mantellum, cuculla, and caputium.

4. ANTONIUS, ST (*Canons of*).—Black gown signed with a blue T; girded white collar, black mantle, also signed with T. Others, who are devoted to manual labour, wear a similar dress, but tawny in colour. The T is a representation of a crutch, the symbol of sustaining and power.

5. ANTONIUS, ST (*Egypt*).—Black tunic and scapular, with round caputium. Discalced.

6. ANTONIUS, ST (*Syria*).—Long black gown with short round caputium, black leather girdle; over all, long black mantle.

7. APOSTOLI.—Tawny tunic with girdle of leather, scapular with caputium attached. Cappa, and in winter short and narrow mantellum.

8. AUBERT, ST (*Canons regular of; Cambrai*).—Violet cassock, and cap or biretta: white surplice.

9. AUGUSTINE, ST.—Black tunic girded, black cape and hood. White may be worn indoors.

10. AVELLANANS.—White tunic, scapular, azure pallium, square biretta in place of mantellum.

11. BASIL, ST (*Armenia*).—Tunic and caputium white, scapular black.

12. BASIL, ST (*Germany*).—Tunic, long scapular, long broad cappa, caputium on shoulder, and a biretta on head in outline resembling the 'Tam o' Shanter' cap.

13. BASIL, ST (*Greece*).—Black woollen tunic, over which another with sleeves about three palms wide, open in front, with woollen fringes or loops of another (but still dark) colour, which can be fastened with small buttons. Head always covered with a cap, which conceals the ears. Caputium with *vittae* or streamers attached, which hang over the shoulders, and are said to typify the cross.

14. BASIL, ST (*Italy or Spain*).—Till 1443 resembling the Greek dress (No. 13). After that date, tunic, leather girdle, scapular, cuculla, caputium—all black.

15. BASIL, ST (*Russia*).—Like Greece (No. 13), with the addition of a small cuculla.

16. BENEDICT, ST (*St Justina of Padua*).—Black woollen tunic to which a caputium is sewn. Scapular; cuculla from shoulder to feet with very wide sleeves.

17. BENEDICT, ST (*Clugniacs*).—Black cappa clausa with rude sleeves or hood.

18. BENEDICT, ST (*India*).—Black tunic somewhat short, white scapular, mantle, and caputium.

19. BETHLEHEMITES.—Black woollen tunic with leather girdle; cappa, on left side of which a *pannula* with a representation of the manger at Bethlehem. Discalced. Black cap on head.

20. BIRGITTA, ST.—Gray tunic and cuculla, to which a caputium is sewn, gray mantellum, signed with red cross, having a white roundle or plate at the centre.

21. CAELESTINES.—White, black caputium and scapular.

22. CAMALDULENSES (*Hermits*).—White woollen tunic, scapular and round caputium; cuculla (also white) in service. Black shoes.

23. CAMALDULENSES (*Monks*).—As Benedictines, but white, and the scapular is girded round the loins. Tunic with very wide sleeves, caputium, etc.

24. CAPUCHINS.—Rough black woollen tunic girded with coarse rope; hood and cape. Discalced.

25. CARMELITES. — Tunic, girdle, scapular, caputium, brown; cappa or mantle white. Hat on head black, except in Mantua, where it is white.

26. CARMELITES A MONTE SACRO. — Cappa shorter than that of the other Carmelites, and no cap on head at any time.

27. CARTHUSIANS.—Black woollen pallium, over which white gown passed over the head, and scapular with side loops.

28. CISTERCIANS.—Benedict XII decreed *brown* as the Cistercian colour; but there was an uncertainty as to the interpretation of this decree; some, alleging that *gray* or *black* were included in the term 'brown,' wore those colours. To remedy this confusion, Sixtus IV decreed black or white: black caputium and scapular girded round loins; black cuculla added out of doors. In choir white.

29. CISTERCIANS (*Fogliantino*).—Like the Benedictines in shape, white in colour. Formerly discalced everywhere, now only in France. Black wooden sandals worn in Italy.

30. CISTERCIANS (*La Trappe*).—White cuculla with ample sleeves, girded; caputium.

31. CHARITON, ST. — Lion-coloured tunic, with black cuculla and caputium.

32. CHOORS (*Canons regular of; Bordeaux*). — White woollen vestis, white linen scapular; linen cotta in choir. Almuce, worn over the arms in summer, round the neck in winter.

33. COLORITI (*Calabria*).—Long tunic, with round caputium and mantellum from rough black natural wool; woollen girdle.

34. COLUMBA, ST (*Avellana*). — White woollen tunic or caputium, over which a scapular; a narrow pallium added out of doors.

35. CROSS, ST (*Canons regular of; Coimbra*).—Cassock, surplice, and almuce; the ordinary canonical dress.

36. CRUCIFERS (*Italy*).—Blue tunic (formerly ash-coloured, or uncertain), scapular, and hood. Silver cross constantly borne in the hand.

37. CRUCIFERS (*Belgium*). — White tunic, scapular, and caputium; black mozetta, signed in front with a red and white cross.

Costumes of the Religious Orders. 239

38. CRUCIFERS (*Lusitania*).—Blue tunic, over which gown, mozetta and hood. A pallium added out of doors.

39. CRUCIFERS (*Syria*).—Black.

40. DIONYSIUS, ST (*Canons regular of; Rheims*).—Long surplice, over which (in winter) a cappa clausa without armholes. Biretta. Almuce worn over arm.

41. DOMINIC, ST.—Tunic, scapular, and broad round caputium of white wool. Black cappa, shorter than the tunic, added out of doors.

42. FONTIS EBRALDI (*Fontevraud*).—Black tunic girded, scapular, caputium.

43. FRANCIS, ST.—Ash-coloured tunic girded with a cord divided by three knots; round caputium and mozetta.

44. FRANCIS, ST (*de observantia*).—Woollen tunic girded with cord; cape, hood; colour formed by mixture of two parts of black wool to one of white. Discalced, in wooden or leathern sandals.

45. FRANCISCANS (*of St Peter of Alcantara*).—Rough and patched tunic girded with cord; cape and hood. Feet entirely unprotected.

46. FRANCIS DE PAUL, ST (*Fratres minimi*).—Woollen tunic, dark tawny colour with round caputium, whose ends hang below the loins before and behind, both girded by a rope, the free end of which is knotted with five knots (novices knot *three* knots only). Pallium reaching a little below the knees, worn in winter both indoors and out. Formerly discalced, with sandals of various materials; afterwards, however, this practice was dispensed with.

47. GENOVEFA, ST (*Canons regular of*).—White vestis and rochet, black biretta, fur almuce over left arm. In winter a long black pallium is added to the vestis and rochet, and a black caputium or hood.

48. GEORGE IN ALGA, ST (*Canons regular of*).—Cassock, over which a blue gown.

49. GILBERT, ST (*Canons regular of*).—Black cassock and

hood, and surplice lined with lamb's wool. Linen cappa added at service.

50. GRAMONTANS.—Any dress, very rough. The 're-formed' dress is a rough white linen tunic, over which another, thinner, of black; scapular and caputium.

51. HERMITS (*Egypt*).—Tawny tunic, black pallium.

52. HIPPOLYTUS, St (*Brothers of Mercy of*).— Brownish tunic, scapular, hood.

53. HUMILIATI.—White tunic, scapular, mantle, cape, and cap.

54. JAMES, ST (*Canons regular of; Spada*).—White woollen vestis and rochet.

55. JEROME, ST (*Hermits of*). — White woollen tunic, scapular with round caputium, cappa open in front : all black wool.

56. JEROME, ST (*Hermits of; foundation of Lupo Olmedo*).— White tunic girt with black leather girdle round loins; small round caputium and tawny cuculla. Black biretta worn at home.

57. JEROME, ST (*Hermits of; foundation of Peter Gambacorta*). —Tawny tunic girded with leather girdle, tawny crimped cappa, round and narrow caputium, square black biretta.

58. JEROME, ST (*Fiesole*). — Tawny woollen vestis with crimped cappa open in front. Leather girdle. Discalced; wooden sandals, afterwards abandoned.

59. JESUATI.—White tunic, square caputium, gray cappa (after 1367). A white appendage, like a sleeve, worn instead of caputium, changed by Urban VIII for a caputium of the same colour as the mantle.

60. JOHANNIS DEI, ST.—Dark ash-coloured tunic with scapular reaching to knees;* round, pointless caputium. Black cap added out of doors.

---

* So Bonanni's text; it reaches to the *feet* in his plate.

61. JOHN, ST (*Canons regular of; Chartres*).—White vestis and rochet; almuce over left shoulder.

62. JOHN, ST (*Hermits of, de Pœnitentia*).—Rough woollen cloth, tunic and cappa with hood, feet entirely unprotected, heavy wooden cross suspended in front from neck.

63. JOHN BAPTIST, ST (*Canons regular of; England*).—Black or brown vestis, scapular, cappa clausa, and mantle, all signed with a black cross.

64. KLOSTERNEUBURG (*Canons regular of; Austria*).—White surplice and black cappa, for which latter an almuce is substituted on festival days.

65. LIRINENSES (*Lerina Island, Tuscany*).—Tunic and mantle girded with scarf, over this sleeved cappa aperta with small caputium: all black.

66. LO, ST (*Canons regular of; Rouen*).—Violet cappa, violet mozetta or cape, and hood in winter; white cassock and rochet.

67. MACHARIUS, ST (*Egypt*).—Violet tunic, black scapular, small cuculla; cap on head covering hair, forehead, temples, and ears.

68. MARK, ST (*Canons regular of; Mantua*).—White woollen vestis, rochet, pallium, for which latter a mozetta is substituted in choir and a white biretta added. Sheepskin almuce on left arm.

69. MARTIN, ST (*Esparnai* [*Aspreniacum, Campania*]).— Vestis talaris of white, above which a sarrocium or scorligium, which is a species of rochet, described by Mauburnus.*

---

* Cit. ap. Bonanni, vol. iv, No. xvii: Quidam enim subtile integrum cum manicis integris habent, quidam autem deferunt hanc lineam vestem in formam longi et lati scapularis sine manicis in lateribus apertam quidam circa tibia ad latitudinem palmae Carthusiensium more consutam, alii scapulare latum cum rugis habent aliis est forma parvi scapularis et brevis cum rugis et plicis e collo pendentis quod Scorligium

70. MARY, ST (*de Mercede Redemptionis Captivorum*).—
White tunic, scapula, short caputium, and cappa. A small
shield bearing *party per fess in chief gules a cross pattée argent
in base three pallets* (the base charge is the arms of the
Kingdom of Arragon), is worn in front.

71. MARY, ST (*de Mercede Redemptionis Captivorum, another
dress*). — In this the caputium is prolonged and the feet
discalced.

72. MARY, ST (*Servants of*).—Coarse tunic, scapular, cappa
and hood : all black.

73. MAURICE, ST (*Canons regular of*).—Cassock, rochet,
purple cape or mozetta, biretta.

74. MONTE LUCA (*Hermits of*).—Tunic, short chasuble-
like scapular, mantle and hood and cap or hat, the latter
optional ; all tawny colour. Some are discalced, others with
shoes or sandals.

75. MONTE SENARIO (*Hermits of*).—Black tunic, scapular,
pallium extending below knees, caputium.

76. MONTE VERGINE (*in Avellina; monks of*). — Tunic,
scapular, and cuculla ; out of doors pallium and cap substituted for cuculla. All white.

77. OLIVETANS.—White vestis with wide sleeves, caputium
crispatum on shoulder.

78. PACHOMIUS, ST.—White woollen tunic and cuculla, the
latter signed with a violet cross.

79. PAMPLONA (*Canons regular of*).—Cassock, alb, sleeveless
rochet, ash-coloured mozetta.

80. PAUL, ST (*Hermits*).—White woollen vestis, rather
short, with short mantellum over, and short caputium ;
discalced.

81. PAUL, ST (*Monks*).—White tunic sleeved, caputium,

---

dicunt quibusdam ex latere linea hasta aliis arca collum pecia
linea.

and collar round shoulders. Out of doors, black cap and cloak (white in Hungary).

82. PETER, ST (*Canons regular of; Monte Corbulo*).—At first gray cassock and rochet, and almuce or caputium; after 1521 black cassock, white-sleeved rochet, and black cloak.

83. POLAND (*Canons regular of*).—White tunic and linen surplice reaching to about the knees, fur almuce about shoulders, dark-coloured skull-cap of wool edged with fur.

84. PORTUGAL (*Canons regular of*). — White rochet and tunic, tawny almuce, and pallium.

85. PRÆMONSTRATENSIANS.—White tunic and scapular, sewn up in front, white sleeveless cappa without girdle, white biretta, almuce, white shoes. (The white is all *natural*, not dyed.)

86. ROUEN (*Canons regular of the Priory of the Two Lovers*). —White tunic or alb and rochet, almuce.

87. RUFUS, ST (*Canons regular of; France*).—White cassock buttoned up in front, white girdle, black biretta.

88. SABBA, ST.—Tawny tunic girded, with black scapular. Discalced.

89. SAVIOUR, ST (*Canons regular of; Laterans*).—White buttoned cassock, linen rochet. Out of doors black pallium and biretta.

90. SAVIOUR, ST (*Canons regular of; Lorraine*).—Black tunic with little linen rochet hanging down from the neck to the left side, five inches broad, like a girdle, over which in choir a cotta, and gray almuce carried on the arm in summer; in winter a full sleeveless rochet with cappa reaching to the ankles of black linen, whose front edges are decorated with red cloth about a foot wide. Caputium, whose front edge surrounds the face like an almuce, with fur about two inches wide.

91. SAVIOUR, ST (*Canons regular of; Sylva Lacus Selva*).— White woollen tunic, rochet and scapular, black cappa.

92. SEPULCHRE, THE HOLY (*Canons regular of*).—White

rochet, black cappa and caputium. At the left side of the cappa a Greek cross cantoned by crosslets in red.

93. SEPULCHRE, THE HOLY (*Canons regular of; Bohemia, Poland, Russia*).—Black vestis and rochet, over which a mantelletum—a waistcoat or rochet-like vestment, sleeveless, but rather long, open in front, and reaching to a little above the knees—on the left side of which a double-transomed cross.

94. SYLVESTER, ST.—Tunic, caputium, scapular, cuculla of blue. Biretta worn on sacred occasions.

95. TRINITATIS, SS (*Redemptionis Captivorum*).—White tunic, scapular, and cappa, with red and blue cross flory on the scapular and left side of the cappa.

96. TRINITATIS, SS (*Redemptionis Captivorum; Spain*).— Cappa brown, otherwise as above described. By others in Spain a tawny cappa is worn, and the feet are discalced. Round black caputium added.

97. TRINITATIS, SS (*Redemptionis Captivorum; France*).— All white, the cross plain; feet discalced; caputium also white.

98. USETZ (*Canons regular of*).—White buttoned tunic and surplice, extinguisher-shaped, like the ancient chasuble.

99. VALLE DE CHOUX (*Burgundy, between Dijon and Autun, Canons regular of*).—White, black scapular, girded with black girdle.

100. VALLE RONCEAUX (*Canons regular of*).—Black, with white scapular, very small, and resembling archiepiscopal pall. Black cappa added in service.

101. VALLE DI SCHOLARI (*Canons regular of*).—White woollen tunic and scapular; black cappa lined with lamb's wool, biretta.

102. VALLEY OF JEHOSHAPHAT (*Canons regular of*).—Full red cuculla and caputium.

103. VALLIS VIRIDIS (*near Brussels; Canons regular of*).— Black tunic and cassock, white rochet, black caputium.

104. VALLUMBROSANS.—Identical with the Sylvestrines, but grayish-black instead of blue.

105. VICTOR, ST, WITHOUT THE WALLS (*Canons regular of; Paris*).—White tunic and wide-sleeved surplice, almuce, biretta.

106. VINDESHEIM (*Canons regular of*).—White tunic and rochet, biretta, fur almuce added on shoulders in winter.

107. WILLIAM, ST (*Hermits of*). — Tunic, over which another sleeveless, girded. Scapular, feet entirely unprotected. At first white, but black after union with the Augustinians.

Nuns.

The dress of nuns, as a general rule, consists of a *vestis* (gown or tunic), girt at the waist, and a scapular. To these various orders add *pallia, mantella*, etc., as will appear from the following list. As a general rule, a white *gremial* or breastcloth is fastened over the head and round the throat and breast; over this two loose *vela* or cloths are placed on the head, the inner white, the outer black. The feet, even of 'discalced' nuns, are protected at least by wooden, bark, or leathern sandals; very rarely are the feet entirely unprotected.

1. ACEMETAE (*or Vigilants*). — Uncertain; according to some authorities, green vestis, signed with a red cross, above which a mantellum or cape. Black velum on head.

2. AGNES, ST (*Dordrecht*).—White vestis and scapular, black velum on head, ruff round neck.

3. AMBROSE, ST.—White, black velum on head.

4. ANGELICA, ST (*Milan*).—White vestis and scapular, cross on breast, ring on finger, with cross in place of a jewel.

5. ANTONIUS, ST (*Syria*).—No definite rule, any dress suitable to monastic life.

6. AUGUSTINE, ST (*Solitaries of*, 1256).—Black; Gregory IX gave licence to wear white, with black scapular and velum on head.

7. AUGUSTINE, ST (*ancient habit*).—Black tunic, white linen rochet, on head a cloth, ornamented with semée of red crosses, reaching down the back like a cloak or cope.

8. AUGUSTINE, ST (*discalced; Spain*).—Similar to the corresponding monks, but with the usual vela on the head.

9. AUGUSTINE, ST (*discalced; Lusitania*).—White vestis (to which a black vestis is added on feast days) girded with black leather girdle, white scapular, black mantellum; on the head a rough white linen cloth hanging before the face to the eyes, but behind to the waist. On this white cloth another, black, about five palms in breadth.

10. AUGUSTINE, ST (*Penitents of*).—Black vestis and cappa, reaching to knees; scapular white; face covered with a black veil.

11. AUGUSTINE, ST (*Venice*).—White; black veil on face.

12. BASIL, ST (*Eastern*).—Natural (undyed) black dress; black mafors (narrow scapular-like pallium); gloves or sleeves covering the arms and hands as far as the fingers; black velum covering the whole head.

13. BASIL, ST (*Western*).—As in the East till 1560. After that date, black vestis, scapular and velum reaching from head to knees; black gremial or breast-cloth. A cassock with ample sleeves added for church services.

14. BEGGA, ST (*Antwerp*).—Black vestis, black pallium from head downwards, a cap (biretta), resembling in outline an inverted saucer, on head white velum round head and across breast.

15. BENEDICT, ST.—As monks, but with velum in place of caputium.

16. BENEDICT, ST (*de Monte Calvario*).—White tunic and scapular, with black velum on head. Discalced.

17. BIRGITTA, ST.—White camisia, gray tunic, cuculla with sleeves reaching to tip of middle finger, gray mantellum. On the head a 'garland' or 'wreath' concealing the forehead and cheeks, and secured at the back of the head by a pin

Costumes of the Religious Orders. 247

On this is placed a black velum fastened by three pins, one on the forehead and one over each ear. Above this is a corona of white cloth consisting of a Greek cross passing over the head from forehead to back and from ear to ear, the ends joined by a circle that passes round the temples. At each of the intersections of the cross arms with each other and with the circle is fastened a small piece (*gutta*) of red cloth—the total of five doubtless typical of the Five Wounds.

18. CAESARIUS, ST.—White vestis, girded; black velum on head.

19. CALATIAVANS.—White; white scapular signed with red cross flory, usual white and black vela on head.

20. CAMALDULENSES.—White; scapular confined with white girdle; usual vela on head.

21. CANONESSES REGULAR (*Belgium, Lorraine*, etc.).—White tunic girt at waist, mantle over; black velum on head; a rochet is worn in some houses.

22. CANONESSES REGULAR (*Rouen*).—Originally white; now black tunic, black mantellum lined and edged with white mouse-fur; black and white vela disposed as usual on head.

23. CANONESSES (*Mons*).—Black vestis with white sleeves; black velum on head reaching down back half-way; pallium or mantle on shoulder hanging to ground, black lined with white. In church service the dress consists of white linen surplice or cassock reaching to feet, braided with a cord sewn upon it arranged in ornamental knots and scrolls; peaked head-dress, from the point of which hangs a long pendant streamer. Pallium or mantle of black silk, lined with mouse-fur, white with black spots.

24. CAPUCHINS. — Rough woollen vestis, scapular, mantellum, white gremial cloth, black and white vela on head.

25. CARMELITES (*ancient*). — Tawny tunic, short white pallium or mantle, white velum encircling head.

26. CARMELITES (*modern*).—Tawny tunic and scapular, white pallium reaching to feet, usual vela on head.

27. CARMELITES (*France*).—Brown habit, white mantellum lined with fur, white gremial cloth covering head and breast, black velum above this.

28. CARMELITES (*discalced*).— Like ordinary Carmelites, but with somewhat long cappa of coarse cloth ; two black vela on head ; feet shod with woollen cloth and bark sandals.

29. CARTHUSIANS.— White tunic and scapular ; cloth on neck and breast, usual velamina on head.

30. CASSIAN.—White tunic and linen rochet, with black velum on head.

31. CISTERCIANS.—White ; gray (sometimes black) scapular, girded ; in choir a white cuculla added.

32. CLUGNIACS.—Black tunic, girded ; ample scapular, also black ; usual vela on head.

33. COLUMBANUS, ST.—White tunic, cuculla, gremial cloth, and velum on head.

34. CROSS, ST (*Penitents of*).—White tunic, over which another, black, girded with leather girdle. White gremial cloth and velum.

35. DOMINIC, ST.—White vestis, girded ; scapular ; black and white vela on head. In choir or at the Sacrament a cappa is added.

36. DOMINIC, ST (*Penitents of*).—White tunic and scapular ; white gremial cloth and velum, over which a flowing black pallium is placed which hangs down to the feet.

37. ELIGIUS, ST.—Black tunic, white mantle, white gremial cloth on head and breast, over which black velum.

38. FONTEVRAUD.—Black tunic, white gremial and velum.

39. FONTEVRAUD (*reformed*). — Black pallium added to previous dress.

40. FRANCIS OF ASSISI, ST.—Rough tunic girt with a rope, scapular and mantellum ; white gremial cloth. Discalced ; feet in wooden sandals.

41. FRUCTUOSUS, ST. — Cuculla, pallium, and tunic, all

gray; girdle securing tunic black. Discalced (sandals worn in summer, shoes in winter).

42. GENOVEFA, ST (*Canonesses of*).—White tunic and surplice, black fur 'almutia,' ornamented with white spots, worn at service over left arm (something like a long maniple). White gremial cloth, and black velum over it on head.

43. GILBERT, ST.—Black tunic, mantle, and hood, the last lined with lamb's wool.

44. HILARY, ST.—Gray tunic, not long, over which a short tawny pallium; black velum on head, with white band round forehead; shoes with pointed toes turned upward.

45. HOSPITALERS OF ST JOHN OF JERUSALEM. — Tawny tunic with white cross sewn on breast. White velum on head.

46. HOSPITALERS OF ST JOHN OF JERUSALEM (*France*).— Black vestis signed with a white cross fourchée; pallium with similar cross on left shoulder; white and black vela on head. Fastened to the pallium a rosary divided into eight parts, symbolical of the instruments of the Passion.

47. HOSPITALERS (*Canonesses; Paris*).—White vestis, linen rochet, pallium from shoulders to feet, usual vela on head.

48. HOSPITALERS OF THE HOLY GHOST (*Saxony*).—Black vestis, with double-transomed cross fourchée in white on the left side of breast. Usual vela on head.

49. HUMILIATI (*Milan*).—White tunic girded; loose white scapular; white velum.

50. INFANT JESUS, VIRGINS OF.—Woollen vestis of dark tawny colour. On certain days black velum on head reaching nearly to feet.

51. ISIDORE, ST. — Uncertain; probably gray tunic and cappa with hood. Discalced.

52. JAMES, ST, DE SPATHA.—Black vestis with red cross flory fichée on the right on the breast. White cappa reaching to feet. Usual vela on head.

53. JEROME, ST. — White tunic, gray scapular, black pallium, black velum on head.

54. JESUATAE.—White tunic and brown scapular; cappa of the same colour added at service. Usual vela on head.

55. LATERAN CANONESSES REGULAR.—White tunic and rochet; white gremial cloth over head and breast, over which black velum. A wide-sleeved surplice added for service.

56. LAURENCE, ST (*Venice*).—Black vestis with white velum on head, not altogether covering the hair. A long flowing cassock added for a service-robe, and a long black velum placed over the white velum.

57. MACHARIUS, ST.—Tawny vestis with black cappa, or a sheepskin over it.

58. MALTA, KNIGHTS OF.—Black tunic and scapular, black pallium, very long and supported over the arms to keep it from the ground; white Maltese cross on left shoulder of pallium. Black and white silk chain hanging from neck supporting wooden images of the instruments of the Passion.

59. MARIA, ST, IN CAPITOLIO (*Canonesses of*).—Silk vestis, above which a white rochet. Head covered with long black velum reaching to ground. At first a crimped, ruff-like collar round the neck; this was afterwards abandoned.

60. MARIA FULIENSIS, ST. — Rough white vestis; white gremial cloth on head and breast, loosely covered with black velum. Discalced.

61. MARY THE VIRGIN, ST, ANNUNCIATION OF.—Gray tunic, white chlamys or cloak, red cross-shaped scapular, usual head coverings.

62. MARY THE VIRGIN, ST, ANNUNCIATION OF (*another order*). —White vestis, black girdle, white scapular, blue gown, white gremial on head and breast, black velum.

63. MARY THE VIRGIN, ST, ASSUMPTION OF.—Blue, secured with white girdle, white scapular, white gremial cloth, white velum (very long) on head. In choir a pallium of mixed silk and blue wool is added.

64. MARY THE VIRGIN, ST (*Canonesses regular of*).—Black

tunic, over which a long black cappa is girded in choir; usual gremial cloth and vela.

65. MARY THE VIRGIN, ST, DAUGHTERS OF (*Cremona*).—Black. Resembling the habit of the priests of the Society of Jesus, but with black velum in place of biretta. An extra black velum and an extra black mantle is added out of doors.

66. MARIA, STA (*de Mercede Redemptionis Captivorum*).—White vestis and scapular; usual vela on head. In centre of breast a shield bearing *party per fess in chief gules a cross pattée argent, in base three pallets*.

67. MARY THE VIRGIN, ST, SERVANTS OF.—Same as corresponding monks, with velum instead of caputium. In Germany certain of this order wear a white velum with a blue star on the forehead.

68. MARY THE VIRGIN, ST, SEVEN SORROWS OF.—Black woollen vestis and girdle, head and breast with white linen covering, long black head-covering put on out of doors.

69. MARY THE VIRGIN, ST, PURIFICATION OF.—Simple black vestis, white collar and cuffs, black velum on head—much like ordinary mourning dress.

70. MARY THE VIRGIN, ST, VISITATION OF.—Black vestis, pectoral cross of silver with figure and monogram of Christ. Usual vela on head.

71. MARY OF THE ROSARY, ST.—Black; image of the Conception, surrounded by a rosary embellished with figures of the instruments of the Passion, on breast; white gremial cloth and white velum on head.

72. OLIVETANS.—White cuculla and tunic; usual vela on head.

73. PACHOMIUS, ST.—Black tunic and gray hood; a row of small white Greek crosses along every edge.

74. PHILIPPINES OF ROME. — Black woollen tunic, white sleeveless surplice with black cross in centre. Usual vela on head.

75. PRÆMONSTRATENSIANS.—White vestis and pallium, white

scapular girded. On the forehead a cross signed on the white velum.

76. PETER OF ALCANTARIA, ST (*Solitaries of*).—Rough vestis girded with a rope ; scapular, mantle, and velum. No covering on head.

77. SACRAMENT, ADORATION OF THE MOST HOLY.—Black vestis, black velamen over head and shoulders, golden figure of the Host on breast.

78. MARY THE VIRGIN, ST, PRESENTATION OF.—Black, white scapular, usual vela on head signed with cross in the centre of the forehead.

79. SEPULCHRE, CANONESSES OF THE HOLY.—Black tunic, over which a white sleeveless surplice reaching to knees. Usual vela on head. Mantellum, on the left shoulder of which is a double transomed cross in red. To the left side are two ropes sewn, knotted together by five knots to typify the Five Wounds.

80. STEPHEN, ST.—White woollen vestis and scapular with red cross fourchée on breast. Usual vela on head. In choir a white cuculla is added with full sleeves of red silk.

81. SYLVESTER, ST.—Similar to monks, but with usual vela on head.

82. TRINITATIS, SS (*Redemptionis Captivorum*).—White vestis and scapular, black pallium. On pallium and scapular a red and blue Greek cross fourchée. Usual vela.

83. TRINITY, MOST HOLY.—White tunic and scapular, tawny cappa signed with Greek cross fourchée in red and blue. Similar cross on scapular. Black sandals.

84. URBANISTS.—Blackish vestis and scapular, tawny mantellum at service, white gremial cloth, white and black vela on head.

85. URSULA, ST.—Black vestis girded with cord, white gremial cloth, long black velum on head.

86. URSULA, ST (*Rome*).—Woollen vestis of mingled black and violet, with black tunic fastened by black leather

girdle. Usual vela on head, the black one reaching to the knees.

87. URSULA, ST (*Parma*).—Black vestis, very long dark violet pallium, the hem girt up in the girdle, and that part over the head concealing the eyes.

88. VALLUMBROSANAE.—As monks, but with black cuculla usual vela on head.

89. MINISTRANTES INFIRMIS (*Belgium*).—Black dress and scapular; white velum over head and shoulders.

90. MINISTRANTES INFIRMIS (*Liburni*). — Blue dress with long and wide sleeves, white velamen over head and breast, another white velamen loose on head girded with rope round waist.

91. SACRAMENT, POOR VIRGINS OF THE HOLY.—Woollen tawny tunic girt with rope. White velamen on head.

MEDIAEVAL UNIVERSITY COSTUME.

THE details here given respecting mediaeval university costume are abridged from a long and exhaustive paper by Prof. E. C. Clark in vol. 50 of the *Archaeological Journal*.

There is no doubt that the university dress of the middle ages is an adaptation of monastic costume. The original schools from which the universities were developed were of a clerical character, and their members wore clerical dress. The dress of the mediaeval universities was international, unlike the costume worn to-day; hence the following account, while primarily concerned with the English universities, will serve as a description of Continental university dress as well.

The system of degrees was developed in France by the end of the thirteenth century. There were four grades: first, the ordinary scholar or undergraduate; then the determinant; thirdly the licentiate; and fourthly the master, professor or doctor. The undergraduate resided, attended lectures, and argued on questions in the schools; the determinant 'determined' or decided on questions upon which he had previously merely argued; the licentiate received the chancellor's 'licence' to incept (*i.e.*, take the steps necessary for obtaining the master's degree), to lecture, and to dispute in school exercises. The mastership was the highest grade, and it included the regent, who was engaged in teaching, and the non-regent, who had ceased to teach. From the second grade probably sprung the baccalaureat; the bachelor was at first a kind of supernumerary teacher, whose lectures were probably recognised only within his own university.

The robes are thus described:

1. *Toga* or *roba talaris*, the simplest and most general form of university dress, probably originally derived from the Benedictine habit. It was full and flowing, open in front, with wide sleeves through which the arms passed their whole length. Subsequent modifications curtailed the sleeves for undergraduates (retaining the fuller form for mourning), and (in England) introduced distinctive marks for the various colleges. The modern Bachelor and Master of Arts gown is derived from this dress combined with other garments. In certain colleges in Oxford it was directed to be sewn up from the wearer's middle to the ground. In Clare Hall, Cambridge, fellows were permitted to line it with fur. *Gona* and *Epitogium*, which we meet with in certain mediaeval statutes, are probably synonyms of this.

2. *Hood.* The hood (*caputium*) was originally the head-covering in bad weather; it was afterwards dropped on the shoulders, and then assumed the form of a small cape. A large *tippet* is sometimes seen beneath this cape in representations of academical costume. The *Undergraduate's* or *Scholar's hood* was black, not lined, and to it a long liripipe or streamer was sewn at the back; the *Graduate's* was furred or lined, with a short liripipe. The various degrees were indicated by differences of lining; bachelors wore badger's fur or lamb's

Mediaeval University Costume. 255

wool; licentiates and regents wore minever or some more expensive fur; non-regents wore silk. When the undergraduates abandoned hoods (before sixteenth century; exact date uncertain) they became a distinctive mark of the attainment of a degree.

The liripipe was also called *tipetum* or *cornetum*. The latter may be the origin of the French *cornette*, a silk band formerly worn by French doctors of law, and a possible origin for the modern English scarf. The word *liripipe* is also used to denote pendant false sleeves, and also the tails of long-pointed shoes. This, however, lies rather in the region of everyday costume. In 1507, at Oxford, we find *typet* or *cornetum* used to denote an alternative for the *toga talaris* allowed to Bachelors of Civil Law. This is clearly not the tail of a hood, but its exact significance is uncertain.

3. *Mantellum.* The origin and meaning of this word are alike uncertain. The use of '*mantelli* or *liripipia*, commonly called typets,' was prohibited to fellows and scholars of Magdalen College, Oxford, by a statute dated 1479, except *infirmitatis causa*. From this we may infer that the *mantellus* (also called *mantella* or *mantellum*) was something akin to the liripipe. In another notice (1239) they are coupled with *cappae*: certain riotous clerks had to march in a penitential procession '*sine cappis et mantellis*.' Prof. Clark infers from these passages and from other sources that the academical mantellum 'is not a hood, but is worn either instead of, or in addition to, the hood, with the cope, or else instead of the cope or long tabard.'

4. *Cassock.* This was at one time worn by all members of universities under their gowns. Doctors of divinity, doctors of laws, cardinals, and canons wore scarlet. Certain days at present are called 'Scarlet Days' in the English universities, on which doctors in all faculties wear scarlet. This may be a survival of the ancient scarlet cassock.

5. *Surplice.* 'A dress of ministration, used in college

chapels by non-ministrants, more as a matter of college discipline than as academical costume.'

6. *Almuce.* Distinctive of masters and doctors, distinct from the hood. Another possible origin of the English hood.

7. *Cope.* There were two kinds of cope in use at the English universities—the *cappa manicata* or sleeved cope; and an uncomfortable contrivance called the *cappa clausa*, which was sewn all the way up, passed over the head when put on, and was not provided with sleeves or other openings for the arms save a short longitudinal slit in front. The Archbishop of Canterbury prescribed this as a decent garb for Archdeacons, Deans and Prebendaries in 1222. Regents in arts, laws, and theology were permitted to lecture in a *cappa clausa* or *pallium* only. The *cappa manicata* was probably worn generally, as being a sober and dignified dress; it very rarely occurs in contemporary representations.

8. The *tabard* or *colobium* was a sleeveless gown closed in front; but ultimately it was slit up, the sleeves of the gown proper were transferred to it, and the use of the latter discontinued. All not yet bachelors were required by the statutes of Trinity Hall, Cambridge (1352), to wear long tabards, while Clare Hall, the adjoining foundation, required its Master (Head), masters, and Bachelor Fellows to wear this and other robes, in 1359. Kings' Hall (1380) required every scholar to wear a *roba talaris*, and every bachelor a robe with tabard suited to his degree.

9. *University Head-dress.* A skull-cap was early allowed to ecclesiastics to protect the tonsured head in cold weather, and, except the ordinary hood, this is the only head-dress recognised by the early university statutes. This *pileus*, however, soon assumed a pointed shape, thus ⌒ and in this form was recognised as part of the insignia of the doctorate; doctors only are represented wearing it upon monuments. The central point developed afterwards into the modern tassel. Bachelors wore no official head-dress.

APPENDIX II.

AN INDEX OF SYNONYMOUS TERMS.

Alba (Lat.), alb.
Ἀναβολάδιον (Gk.), amice.
Anabolagium (Lat.), amice.
Ἀναβολαῖον (Gk.), amice.
Anagolaium (Lat.), amice.
Aurifrigium (Lat.), orphrey.
Baltheus (Lat.), girdle.
Bitarshil (Copt.), stole.
Caligae (Lat.), stockings.
Cambo (Lat.), pastoral staff.
Cambutta (Celto-Lat.), head of pastoral staff.
Campagi (Lat.), stockings.
Cappa (Lat.), cope.
Capuita (Lat.), pastoral staff.
Cassacca (Lat.), cassock.
χαμαλαύχιον (Gk.) = χαμαλαύχη.
Chirothecae (Lat.), gloves.
Chrysoclave (O.-Eng., from Lat.), orphrey.
Cingulum (Lat.), girdle.
Clappe (O.-Eng.), pastoral staff.
Cleykstaff (O.-Eng.), pastoral staff.
Cleystaff (O.-Eng.), pastoral staff.
Cruche (O.-Eng.), pastoral staff.

Ephod (Lat., from Heb.), amice.
ἐπιμάνικα (Gk.), maniples.
ἐπιμανικία (Gk.), maniples.
ἐπιτραχήλιον (Gk.), stole.
Faino (Syr.), chasuble.
Fanon (a), (Lat.), maniple.
Fanon (b), (Lat.), orale.
Ferula (Lat.), pastoral staff.
Fourevre (Fr.), mozetta.
Humerale (Lat.), amice.
Hure (O.-Eng.), ecclesiastical skull-cap.
Jabat (Copt.), alb.
Kerchure (O.-Eng.), amice.
Koutino (Syr.), alb.
Manicae (Lat.), gloves.
μανικία (Gk.), maniples.
Mantile (Lat.), maniple.
Mappula (Lat.), maniple.
ὠράριον (Gk.), stole.
Orarium (Lat.), stole.
Oururo (Syr.), stole.
Pedum (Lat.), pastoral staff.
περιτράχηλι (Gk.), stole.
περιτραχήλιον (Gk.), stole.
φαιλόνιον (Gk.), chasuble.
φαίνολι (Gk.), chasuble.
φαινόλιον (Gk.), chasuble.
φακεώλιον (Gk.), stole.

258 *Ecclesiastical Vestments.*

Phrygium (Lat.), orphrey.
Pluviale (Lat.), cope.
Poderis (Lat.), alb.
Poruche (Rus.), maniple.
Regnum (Lat.), tiara.
Roba (Lat.), university gown.
Roc (A.-S.), tunicle or dalmatic.
Sabatyns ⎫ (O.-Eng.), stockings.
Sabbatones ⎭
Sambuca (Lat.), pastoral staff.
στιχάριον ⎫ (Gk.), alb.
στοιχάριον ⎭
Subtile (Lat.), tunicle.
Succinctorium (Lat.), subcingulum.
Sudarium (Lat.), maniple.

Superhumerale (Lat.), alb.
Tibialia (Lat.), stockings.
Tilsan (Copt.), chasuble.
Toga = university gown.
Toumat (Copt.), alb.
Triregnum (Lat.), tiara.
Tunica alba (Lat.), alb.
Tunica talaris (Lat.), cassock; also university gown.
Tunicella (Lat.), tunicle.
ὑπομανικία (Gk.), maniples.
Varkass = vakass.
Vestment (O.-Eng.), chasuble.
Virga pastoralis (Lat.), pastoral staff.
Zendo (Syr.), maniple.
Zona (Lat.), girdle.

APPENDIX III.

A LIST OF THE PRINCIPAL AUTHORITIES REFERRED TO IN THE COMPILATION OF THIS WORK.

*** As this list is intended as a *guide* to the student rather than as a criterion of the labour involved in writing this volume, it has been reduced by the omission of classical and other texts from which casual quotations have been made, and of many books which the author consulted without obtaining any information of value.

Badger (G. P.), The Nestorians and their Ritual. 2 vols. London, 1852.

Bloxam (M. H.), Companion to the Principles of Gothic Ecclesiastical Architecture. London, 1882.

Bock (F.), Geschichte der liturgischen Gewänder des Mittelalters. 3 vols. Bonn, 1859.

List of Principal Authorities. 259

Bona (J.), Rerum liturgicarum libri duo. 3 vols. Turin, 1747.
Bonanni, Catalogo degli ordini religiosi della chiesa militante. 5 vols. Rome, 1722.
Calderwood (D.), Historie of the Kirk of Scotland. 8 vols. Wodrow Society, Edinburgh, 1842-49.
Carter (J.), Specimens of English Ecclesiastical Costume. London, 1817.
Cripps (H. W.), A Practical Treatise on the Law relating to the Church and Clergy. 6th edition. London, 1886.
Dolby (Anastasia), Church Vestments : their Origin, Use, and Ornament. London, 1868.
Fabric Rolls of York Minster. Surtees Society, Durham, 1859. (Also several other volumes of the publications of this Society.)
Fortescue (E. F. K.), The Armenian Church, founded by St Gregory the Illuminator. London, 1872.
Haines (H.), A Manual of Monumental Brasses. Oxford, 1861.
Harrison (B.), An historical Enquiry into the true Interpretation of the Rubrics in the Book of Common Prayer. London, 1845.
Hart (R.), Ecclesiastical Records of England, Ireland, and Scotland from the Fifth Century till the Reformation. Cambridge, 1846.
Hartshorne (C. H.), English Mediaeval Embroidery. *Archaeological Journal*, vol. i, pp. 318-335, vol. ii, pp. 285-301. 1845-47.
Hefele (C. J.), Beiträge zur Kirchengeschichte, Archäologie und Liturgik. 2 vols. Tübingen, 1864.
Howard (G. B.), The Christians of St Thomas and their Liturgies. Oxford, 1864.
Issaverdens (J.), Armenia and the Armenians. 2 vols. Venice, 1874.
Josephus, Works of, ed. Richter. Leipsig, 1826.

King (J. G.), The Rites and Ceremonies of the Greek Church in Russia. London, 1772.
Labbe (P.), and G. Cossart, Sacrosancta concilia ad regiam editionem exacta. 18 vols. Paris, 1671-72.
Lanigan (J.), An Ecclesiastical History of Ireland. 4 vols. Dublin, 1822.
Marriott (W. B.), Vestiarium Christianum. London, 1868.
Martene (E.) and U. Durand, Thesaurus novus anecdotorum. 5 vols. Paris, 1717.
Maskell, Monumenta ritualia ecclesiae anglicanae. Oxford, 1882.
Migne, Patrologia (almost all quotations from the early church writers are taken from this edition). Paris, 1849-64.
Moleon (le Sieur de), Voyages liturgiques de France. Paris, 1718.
Neale (J. M.), A History of the Holy Eastern Church. 4 vols. London, 1850.
Papal Letters (Calendar of Entries in the Papal Registers relating to Great Britain and Ireland, ed. W. H. Bliss). London, 1893.
Paris (M.), Chronica majora. Ed. Luard. 7 vols. Rolls Series. London, 1872-1883.
Pugin (A. W.), Glossary of Ecclesiastical Ornament and Costume. London, 1868.
Quick (J.), Synodicon in Gallia Reformata; or the Acts, Decisions, Decrees, and Canons of those Famous National Councils of the Reformed Churches in France. 2 vols. London, 1692.
Reichel (O. J.), English Liturgical Vestments in the Thirteenth Century. London, 1895.
Renaudot (E.), Liturgiarum orientalium collectio. Paris, 1716.
Rock (D.), Church of our Fathers. 3 vols. London, 1849-52.

Rock (D.), Textile Fabrics : a Descriptive Catalogue of the Collection of Church Vestments, [etc. in South Kensington Museum]. London, 1870.
Row (J.), The History of the Kirk of Scotland from the Year 1538 to August, 1637. Wodrow Society, Edinburgh, 1892.
Rubenius (A.), De re vestiaria veterum, praecipue de lato clavo. In the *Thesaurus Antiquitatum Romanorum* of J. G. Graevius, vol. vi, col. 913. Leyden, 1697.
Saussay (A. de), Panoplia clericalis libri xv. Paris, 1649.
Shaw (H.), Dresses and Decorations of the Middle Ages. 2 vols. London, 1853.
Smith (W.) and S. Cheetham, A Dictionary of Christian Antiquities. London, 1875.
Stothard (C. A.), Monumental Effigies of Great Britain. 2 vols. London, 1817.
Webb, Sketches of Continental Ecclesiology. London, 1848.
Wey (F.), Rome. London, 1872.
Willemin (N. X.), Monumens français inédits. 2 vols. Paris, 1839.

Reference has also been made to the *Church Times*, the *Builder*, and the principal archaeological periodicals and publications of archaeological societies.

INDEX.

ABSOLUTION, vestments worn at, 223
Acolytes, cassock of, 139
—— insignia of, 213, 214
Aethelwold, benedictional of, 115
Aix-la-Chapelle, chasuble at, 86
Alb. *See also* Alba, 64
—— material and colour of, 65
—— ornamentation of, 66, 151
—— plain, when worn, 67
—— symbolism of, 68, 69
—— dimensions of, 69
—— modifications of, 140, 141
—— contrary to English Church law, 201
—— by whom worn, 214
Alba. *See also* Alb, Dalmatica, Roba Talaris
—— by whom and when worn, 28, 30
—— origin of, 29, 31
—— description of, 30
—— canons respecting, 30
—— ornamentation of, 32, 59
—— baptismal, 36, 37
—— of newly baptized, 171
—— sigillata, bullata, 66
—— in Gallican church, 135
—— Eastern equivalent of, 178
Alcuin (pseudo-) quoted, 34, 64, 69, 77, 89, 96, 103, 111, 149
Almuce, description of, 142
—— distinctions of ecclesiastical rank in, 142
—— derivation of name, 142

Almuce, evolution of, 143-146
—— worn under Eucharistic vestments, 219
—— in the universities, 256
Amalarius of Metz quoted, 52, 68, 77, 89, 92-95, 103, 122
Ambrose cited, 38
Amess. *See* Almuce
Amice, 64
—— origin of, 71
—— how, by whom, and when worn, 71, 214
—— description of, 71
—— symbolism of, 72
—— ornamentation of, 151
—— vakass borrowed from, 188
Amys. *See* Almuce
Anastasius Bibliothecarius quoted, 34
Anglican church, vestments in, 194 *et seqq.*
Apparels, 153
Aquinas, St Thomas, cited, 132
Archdeacons, supposed, in St David's Cathedral, 80
Aregius, Bishop, receives dalmatica, 54
Armenian church, baptismal rite in, 171
—— vestments of, 176 *et seqq.*
Augustine cited, 38
Aurelian, his grant of oraria to the Romans, 38
Autun, MS. at, on vestments of the Gallican church, 29, 135

Autun, Honorius of. *See* Honorius
—— Bishops of, their privileges, 102
Auxanius, circumstances of his receipt of the pallium, 51

Bamberg, Bishops of, their privileges, 102
Bands, origin and development of, 208
—— when worn in Presbyterian church, 209
Baptismal vestments of administrator, 36, 122, 222; of baptized, 171
—— alba, 36
—— stole, 222
Bells and pomegranates, 6
Benedict III, life of, quoted, 66
Benediction of vestments, 212
Biretta, birettum, 150, 201
Bishops, insignia of, 27, 28, 213
—— stole, how worn by, 74
—— dalmatic of, 79
—— wearing archiepiscopal insignia, 102
—— subcingulum once worn by, 107
—— vestments worn by, on different occasions, 221. *See also* under the names of different vestments
Bloxam quoted, 80
Bonanni quoted, Appendix i
Boniface VIII adds crown to tiara, 121
Bonnet of Levitical priest, 5
Brachialia, 122
Braga, Councils of. *See* Council
Breastplate of the ephod, 9
Breeches, 4
Bucer quoted, 195
Bullinger quoted, 104
Buskins. *See* Stockings
Byrrhus, 33

Caligae. *See* Stockings
Calliculae, 59
Canons. *See* Council
Canon's cope, 148, 220
Cap, Levitical, 5
—— ecclesiastical, 149

Cap, Malabar, 177
—— university, 256
Cappa, monastic, 235
—— serica, 148
—— manicata, 256
—— clausa, 256
—— *See also* Cope
Caputium, 235, 254
Cardinals wear scarlet cassock, 139
Carthage, Council of. *See* Council
Cashel, crozier of, 127
Cassianus quoted, 44
Cassikin, 204
Cassock, description of, 138
—— distinction of ecclesiastical rank in, 139
—— modern, 139
—— in Presbyterian church, 207
—— in universities, 255
Casula in Gallican church, 29, 135
—— secular, 43, 44
—— *See also* Chasuble
Celebrant, vestments of, 214
Celestine, Pope, his letter on vestment ritual, 26, 46, 57
Cencio de Sabellis quoted, 107, 108
Chain, golden, 103
Χαμαλαύχη, 176, 188, 234
Chambre, Will. de, quoted, 141
Charles I, his ordinance respecting vestments, 204
Charles the Great, 60
Chasuble (*see also* Planeta), 64
—— materials of, 81
—— eucharistic and processional, 82
—— description and varieties of, 83, 84
—— dimensions of, 86
—— ornamentation of, 86, 152
—— symbolism of, 89
—— forbidden in English church, 201
—— folded, when worn, 215
Childebert consents to bestowal of pallium, 51
Chimere, 148, 199
Chirothecae. *See* Gloves
Choir, vestments of, 148, 220
Chorkappa, 194

Chrismale, 171
Chrysome, 172
Cicero quoted, 43
Cidaris, 112
Clark, Professor E. C., quoted, 253, *et seqq.*
Clavi, 31, 32, 42, 49, 58, 80
Clement, liturgy of, 15, 19
Coat of fine linen, 4
Collar, Roman, 148
Colobium, 32-36
—— in the universities, 256
Colours, liturgical, unknown in Early church, 58
—— in Western church, 223
—— in Eastern church, 230
Commodus, 33
Consecration of Archbishop Parker, 198
Constantius, 17
Cope, origin of, 146
—— description and material of, 146
—— hood of, 147
—— morse of, 147
—— canon's, 148, 220
—— ornamentation of, 153
—— for most part forbidden in English church, 201
—— worn by minister, 217
—— university, 256
Corinthians, First Epistle to, quoted, 22
Cornette, Cornetum, 255
Coronation robes, 162. *See* Dalmatic, imperial
Cotta, 141
Council, second of Braga, 40
—— fourth of Braga, 40, 41
—— fourth of Carthage, 30
—— of Mayence, 41
—— first of Narbonne, 30
—— fourth of Toledo, 27, 31, 35, 39, 53, 55, 64, 114, 122
—— *See also* Synod
Coverdale, vestments worn by, 198
—— cited, 200
Cross-staff, 125, 130
Crozier. *See* Pastoral staff
Cuthino, 177, 180
Cyprian, St, of Carthage, 33
Cyril, Bishop of Jerusalem, 17

Dalmatic (*see also* Dalmatica), 64
—— derived from alba, 78
—— episcopal and diaconal, 79, 214
—— ornamentation of, 80, 152
—— symbolism of, 79, 81
—— by whom worn, 214
—— imperial, 229
Dalmatica, a vestment in Rome, 29, 45, 53
—— secular, 32
—— Sylvester's decree concerning, 34
—— Isidore on, 35
David wears ephod, 8
Deacon, insignia of, 28, 34, 52, 214
—— when to wear alba, 30
—— Sylvester's decree respecting vestments of, 34, 52
—— stole, how worn by, 74
—— dalmatic of, 79
—— folded chasuble, when worn by, 215
Degrees, Mediæval university, 253
—— how distinguished by dress, 254
De Saussay quoted, 58
Destruction of vestments, 168
Development of vestments, chaps. i-iii *passim*
Doctors of Divinity wear scarlet cassocks, 139
—— —— wear gray almuces, 142
Doeg, 8
Dol, Bishops of, their privileges, 102
Dolby, Mrs, quoted, 69, 144, 149
Dominica in albis depositis, 172
Dorsal orphrey, 88
Doubles, 220
Drawers, 4
Dublin, Synod of. *See* Synod
Duchesne quoted, 50
Dunstan, St, figure of, 97, 116, 118
Durandus quoted, 106, 134, 172
Durham Rites quoted, 167

Eastern Churches, vestments of, chap. v
'Ἐγκόλπιον, 176, 188, 191
Elagabalus, 33

Index. 265

Embroidery. *See* Apparels, Orphreys
—— Oriental, 162
England, excellence of embroidery in, 163
—— destruction of vestments in, 169
—— vestments of church of, 194
Ephod, description of, 6, 7
—— girdle of, 7
—— by whom worn, 8
—— worshipped, 8, 9
—— proper name, 9
—— breastplate of, 9
—— Latin name for amice, 257
'Επιγονάτιον, 108, 176, 186, 191
'Επιμανίκια, 136, 176, 180, 191, 233
Epiphanius quoted, 113
Epitogium, 254
'Επιτραχήλιον, 50, 176, 182, 191, 233
Estla, 190
Eucharistic vestments, chap. iii
—— chasuble, 82
'Εξωχαμαλαύχη, 176, 188, 191
Exodus, book of, quoted, 4-8

Fabius, 33
Fagius quoted, 195
Ferula, 58
Fife, Synod of. *See* Synod
Final period of vestments, chap. iii
Flower of chasuble, 89
Folkestone ritual case, 201
Fountains Abbey mitre, 119

Gallican church, vestments of, 29, 135
Gammadia, 58
Garland, baptismal, 171
Genesis of vestments, chap. i
Geneva gown, 208
Gebrgi quoted, 106
Germanus quoted, 18, 175, 178, 184
Germany, vestments in, 193
Gideon, 8
Girdle, Levitical, 4
—— of ephod, 7
—— ecclesiastical, 64, 70. *See* also ζώνη

Girdle, contrasted with subcingulum, 107, 109
Gloves, 64
—— when recognised as vestments, 121
—— symbolism of, 122
—— ornamentation of, 152
—— by whom worn, 214
Gold plate, apostolic, 112
Golden chain (loop of pall), 103
Gona, 254
Gown, black preaching, 202, 204
—— monastic, 235
—— university. *See* Toga
—— *See also* Geneva gown
Gregory the Great quoted, 28, 45, 51, 52, 104
—— picture of, 54
—— sacramentary of, 55
Gypcière, 108

Headdress, ecclesiastical, 149
—— university, 256
High Priest, vestments of, 6 *et seq.*
Holland, church of, vestments in, 22, 210
Homer cited, 20
Honorius of Autun quoted, 64, 69, 75, 103, 109, 111, 121, 122, 123, 131
Hood of chasuble, 82
—— of cope, 147, 153
—— monastic, 235
—— university, 254
Hope, Mr St John, quoted, 144, 166
Hosea quoted, 8
Humeral orphrey, 88
Hurrâra, 190

Infulae, 118, 129
Innocent III quoted, 58, 64, 69, 75, 89, 96, 103, 107, 131, 134, 225
Innocent IV covets English orphreys, 163
Institution of bishops, 55
Inventory of Boniface VIII, 75
—— Canterbury, 65
—— Dover, 65
—— Lincoln, 81, 129, 158, 166
—— London, St Mary Hill, 141

Inventory of Peterborough, 65, 66, 68
—— Westminster, 65, 70, 218
—— Winchester, 65, 129
Irish crozier, 126, *et seqq.*
Isidore of Seville, 27, 35, 54, 55, 56, 58, 112, 115, 122, 126
Issues of the Exchequer quoted, 164
Ivo of Chartres quoted, 52, 64, 69, 89, 96, 105, 111, 122

James I prescribes vestments for Scotland, 203
Jerome, 15-18, 114
Jewel, Bishop, cited, 104
Jewish vestments, 2-14, 18, 136
Joannes Diaconus, his portrait of Gregory I, 54
John, Bishop of Ravenna, 53
Josephus quoted, 4-10 *passim*
Judges, Book of, 8, 9

Kamelauch, 234
Κίδαρις, 112
Kodi, 177, 186
Κολόβιον. *See* Colobium
Kulpas, 189

Lampridius quoted, 33, 43, 44
Λαμπρός, meaning of, 19
Landulphus, pontifical of, 40
Laoghairé, druids of King, their prophecy, 115, 128
Lector, 213
Leo III, 58
Letters on vestments, 59
Levitical vestments. *See* Jewish
Limerick mitre, 120
Lincolnshire, destruction of vestments in, 170
Lineae = tails of pall, 104
Linen breeches, 4
—— tunic, 4
Liripipe, 254
Liturgical colours. *See* Colours
Liturgy of Clement. *See* Clement
Lituus, 56
Λωρία, 180
Lucca, Bishops of, their privileges, 102
Luther, reformation of, 193

Macarius, 17
Mafors, 246
Maimonides quoted, 4
Malabar vestments, 177 *et seqq.*
Μανδύας, 176, 187, 191, 234
Manicae, 121, 135
Maniple, 64, 180. *See also* Mappula
—— description of, 75
—— symbolism of, 77
—— ornamentation of, 151
—— by whom worn, 214
Mantelletum, 199
Mantellum, 245, 255
Mantle, 210
Manualia, 29, 135
Mappula, a Roman vestment, 29, 45
—— origin of, 52
—— spread of, 53, 54
Marriott quoted, 15, 16, 19, 25, 29, 50, 62, 94, 115, 122
Martene, 29
Mayence, Council of. *See* Council
Menard, 115
Mesnaemphthes, 5
Messesjorta, 194
Messhake, 194
Micah, 8
Minerva Library, pontifical in, 37
Minister, dress and duties of, at mass, 217, 219, 220
Mitre, Levitical, 10
—— ecclesiastical, 64
—— origin of, 112
—— early, 114
—— development of, 116
—— infulae of, 118
—— ornamentation of, 118
—— various kinds of, 119
—— by whom worn, 214
Monastic dress, appendix i
—— —— Eastern, 234
Monuments, etc., cited—
Arundel, 156
Bamberg, 102, 125
Bathampton, 85
Beverley, 71, 157
Birmingham, 145
Broadwater, 156
Caerleon, 49
Cambridge, 150

Index. 267

Monuments, etc., cited—*continued*
Chesham Bois, 172, 173
Cobham, 145
Ely, 74, 133, 202
Fontevraud, 230
Fulbourne, 156
Havant, 156
Hereford, 145, 219
Horsham, 220
Kilkenny, 90
Lübeck, 193
Mayence, 100, 117, 118, 125
Milton, 77
Norwich, 219
Oxford, 125, 145
Randworth, 78
Ravenna, 46
St David's, 80
Salisbury, 117
Sessay, 147
Shelford, Great, 156
Towyn, 71
Wells, 144, 201, 215, 216, 219
Winwick, 83
Worcester, 67
Wyvenhoe, 76
Morse, 110, 147
Mozetta, 142, 148
Msane, 190

Names of vestments, 68
Narbonne, bishop of, rebuked, 26
—— council of. *See* Council
Nestorian vestments, 189
Nicholas I, Pope, 51
Numbers, Book of, quoted, 9

'Ωμοφόριον, 50, 176, 187, 191, 233
Orale, 64, 134, 153
'Ωράριον, 50, 176, 184, 191, 233
Orarium, 27, 28, 47, 73. *See also* Stole
—— derivation of name, 38
—— secular, 38, 49
—— canons respecting, 39, 40, 41
—— origin of, 38, 49, 50
Oriental embroidery, 162
Origin of vestments, chap. i
Ornamentation of vestments, 58, 66, 87, 150 *et seqq.*
Ornaments rubric, 200

Orphreys, 72, 73, 87, 88, 153
Orro, 177, 184
Ostia, Bishops of, their privileges, 102
Ostiarius, 213
Ouches, 7

Paenula, 43, 44, 49, 186
Pall, 64, 187. *See also* Pallium
—— material and development of, 96
—— history of individual specimens, 99
—— by whom and when worn, 96, 100, 102
—— symbolism of, 102
—— cost of, 104
—— not ornamented, 98, 152
Pallium, monastic cloak, 26, 46, 235, 245
—— vestment = pall, 29, 47-51, 135
—— linostimum, 34, 46, 52
Paris, Matthew, quoted, 163
Parker, consecration of Archbishop, 198
Pasbans, 177, 182
Pastoral staff, 27, 64
—— by whom carried, 28, 57, 214
—— origin of, 56
—— description and development of, 57, 126 *et seqq.*
—— erroneous views concerning, 124
—— Irish form of, 126 *et seqq.*
—— infula of, 129
—— symbolism of, 129, 131
Πατέρεσσα, 176, 188, 191
Paul, St, quoted, 22, 35
Pavia, Bishops of, their privileges, 102
Peacock, Mr E., quoted, 170
Pectoral cross, 134, 188, 189, 191
—— orphrey, 88
Pelagians, Jerome's letter against the, 17, 19
Pellicea, 140
Periods of history of vestments, 25
Perizona, 109
Πέταλον, 112, 113

Φαιλόνη, 35
Phaino, 177, 186
Φαινόλιον, 176, 186, 191, 233, 234
Pileus, 151, 256. *See also* Cap
Pins of pall, 97, 98
—— —— symbolism of, 104
Planeta, 28
—— secular, 44
Plate, gold on mitre, Levitical, 10
—— —— apostolic, 112
Plautus quoted, 43
Pollux, Julius, quoted, 43
Polybius cited, 20
Polycrates quoted, 113
Poor-ourar, 176, 184
Pope, grant of pall by, 51, 99, 214
—— his bearing the pastoral staff, 57, 131
—— insignia of, 105, 106, 119, 130, 134, 135, 139, 214
Prayer-Book of 1549, 195
—— 1552, 197
—— 1559, 197
Prazôna, 190
Pre-sanctified, Mass of, 217, 220
Presbyterians, vestments of, 205
Priests, insignia of, 27, 41, 74, 214
Priest's cap, Levitical, 5
Primitive period of vestments, chap. i, 25
Processional vestments, chap. iv
—— chasuble, 82
Pseudo-Alcuin. *See* Alcuin

Rabanus Maurus quoted, 12, 62, 68, 89, 92, 96, 122
Rational, 64, 110-112, 152
Ravenna, mosaics at, 46-48
—— John, Bishop of, 53
Reformed churches, vestments of, chap. vi
Reichel, Rev. O. J., 50
Requiem, vestments worn at, 223
Rhinthon cited, 43
Ring, 54, 64
—— by whom worn, 27, 54, 214, 228
—— description and symbolism of, 123
Ripon Treasurer's Rolls quoted, 174

Ritual uses of vestments, chap. vii
Roba Talaris, 254
Robe of the ephod, 6
Rochet, 141, 199
Rock, Dr, quoted, 48, 49, 66, 67, 75, 85, 106, 108, 114, 115, 134, 135, 144
Roman civil costume, 14 *et seqq.*, chap. ii *passim*
Rubenius, Albertus, quoted, 38
Rulers of the choir, their insignia, 131, 221

Sabanum, 171
Sabellis, Cencio de, 107, 108
Sacramentary of Gregory the Great, 55
Sagavard, 177, 188, 189
Σάκκος, 176, 188, 191, 234
Salisbury missal quoted, 68
Sampson, Thomas, quoted, 199
Samuel, Book of, quoted, 8
—— wears ephod, 8
Sandals, 64
—— development and description of, 90, 91, 95
—— by whom worn, 91, 214
—— symbolism of, 92 *et seqq.*, 96
—— ornamentation of, 91, 152
—— Armenian, 189
Saul, 8
Scapular, 235, 245
Scarf of honour, 38
—— of English church, 203
—— of Presbyterian church, 207
Scarlet days, 255
Scipio, 33
Scotland, vestments in, 203
—— Act of Assembly of church of, 209
Senchus Mór cited, 128
Septuagint cited, 18
Severus, edict concerning paenula, 43
Shaesha, 234
Shapich, 176, 180
Shoes, Malabar, 177
Shoochar, 177, 189
Shorshippa, 190
Simples, 220

Simplicity of early vestments, 11
Sinker, Dr., quoted, 113
Spain, vestments in, 204
Staff. *See* Pastoral Staff
Stockings, 64
—— by whom worn, 105, 214
—— symbolism of, 105
—— ornamentation of, 152
Στοιχάριον, 176, 178, 191, 233
Stola in Gallican church, 29, 135
See also Orarium, Stole
Stole, 64, 182
—— origin of, 72
—— description of, 73, 75
—— how worn, 74, 214
—— symbolism of, 75
—— ornamentation of, 151
—— Spanish, 204
—— worn by kings, 230
—— baptismal, 222
Στολή, 18
Stolone, 215
Subcingulum, 64, 214
—— history of, 106 *et seqq*.
Subdeacons, insignia of, 28, 132, 214
Subiaco, fresco at, 108
Succinctorium. *See* Subcingulum
Sudarium, 50
Superpellicea, 140. *See also* Surplice
Surplice, origin of, 140
—— development and description of, 141
—— varieties of, 141
—— in England, 201
—— in Scotland, 204
—— when worn, 140, 217, 255
Sweden, vestments in, 194
Sylvester, Pope, decree respecting dress, 34-36, 47, 52, 81
Symbolism, 56, 57, 68, 69, 70, 72, 75, 77, 79, 81, 85, 89, 92-96, 102-105, 121, 123, 129, 131, 176, 180, 184, 187
Symmachus grants a pallium, 51
Synagogue models followed by Early Christians, 13
Synod of Dublin, 169
—— Fife, 210

Tabard, 256
Talith, 14
Talmud quoted, 10
Temple worship, 13
Teraphim, 9
Tertullian quoted, 114
Theodore, Archbishop of Laureacus, 51
Theodoret quoted, 17, 18
Thomas of Canterbury, St, his chasuble, 86
Tiara, 112
—— papal, 119, 121
Tippet, 254, 255
Toga, 42, 45, 48
—— university, 254
Toledo, Council of. *See* Council
Transitional period of vestments, chap. ii
Trebellius Pollio quoted, 29
Trèves, Pope bears pastoral staff in, 132
Tunic of linen, 4, 30
—— of blue, 6
—— monastic, 235
Tunica Alba. *See* Alba
—— Dalmatica. *See* Dalmatica
—— Manicata, 32
Tunicle, 64
—— description of, 132
—— by whom worn, 132, 214
—— ornamentation of, 133, 153
—— illegal in English church, 201

University costume, 253
Urban V. adds crown to tiara, 121

Vakass, 176, 188
Valerian quoted, 30
Value of vestments, 164
Vartabeda, insignia of, 189
Velum, 245
—— quadrigesimale, 228
Verona, Bishops of, their privileges, 102
Vestimentum parvolum in Gallican church, 29, 135
Vesting, order of, 217, 231
Vienne, Bishop of, rebuked, 26

Vigilius, grant of a pallium by, 51
Virgilius, Archbishop of Arles, 51
Vopiscus, Flavius, quoted, 38

Walafrid Strabo quoted, 62, 81

Waldenses, vestments among, 206
Zando, 177, 182
Ζώνη, 176, 186, 191, 234
Zosimio, Procurator of Syria, 30
Zunnara, 190
Zunro, 177, 186

THE END.

www.ingramcontent.com/pod-product-compliance
Lightning Source LLC
Chambersburg PA
CBHW032109230426
43672CB00009B/1683